Do You Still Have Time for Chaos?

Also by Lynn Davidson:

Ghost Net
Tender
How to Live by the Sea
Common Land
Islander

Do You Still Have Time for Chaos?

Lynn Davidson

For Em + Dougie
with love

xxx
2024

Te Herenga Waka University Press
PO Box 600, Wellington
New Zealand
teherengawakapress.co.nz

Copyright © Lynn Davidson 2024
First published 2024

This book is copyright. Apart from any fair dealing
for the purpose of private study, research, criticism or review,
as permitted under the Copyright Act, no part
may be reproduced by any process without
the permission of the publishers.
The moral rights of the author have been asserted.

ISBN 9781776921270

A catalogue record is available at the National Library of New Zealand

This book was written with the support of a
Creative New Zealand Randell Cottage residency,
and published with the support of Creative New Zealand

Printed in Singapore by Markono Print Pte Ltd

For Nen & Vida

and for Emily Alison Wigram

Contents

One	The world's end	13
Two	Door into the forest	41
Three	A house in the landscape	65
Four	Disturbing the air	81
Five	These islands	115
Six	Sealskin	147
Seven	An ache for the land	175
Eight	Home	207
Acknowledgements		228
Bibliography		230

John and Helen Johnston

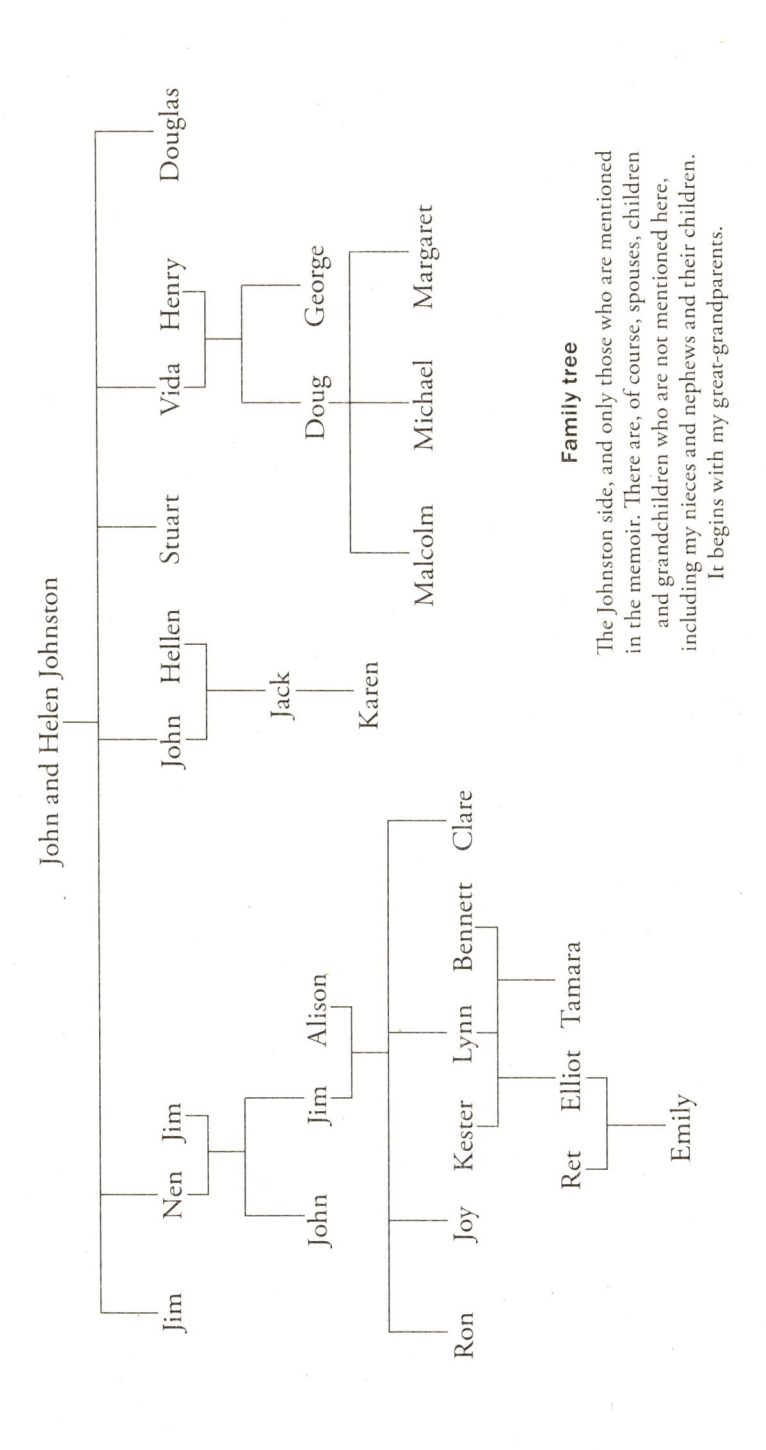

- John — Hellen
  - Jack
    - Karen
- Stuart
- Vida — Henry
  - Doug
  - George
    - Malcolm
    - Michael
    - Margaret
- Douglas

- Jim
- Nen — Jim
  - John
  - Jim — Alison
    - Joy
    - Kester — Lynn
      - Ret
    - Bennett — Clare
      - Elliot — Tamara
        - Emily
- Ron

Family tree

The Johnston side, and only those who are mentioned in the memoir. There are, of course, spouses, children and grandchildren who are not mentioned here, including my nieces and nephews and their children. It begins with my great-grandparents.

Did I disturb ye good people? I hopes I disturb ye, I hopes I disturb ye enough to want to see this, your house, in ruins all around ye! Have you had enough yet? Or do you still have time for chaos?

—Words spoken in court by Temperance Lloyd when she was tried for witchcraft in Devon in 1682

One

The world's end

The world's end

It was eerie to walk the deserted streets of Edinburgh's medieval Old Town and think about those other plague years. They seemed to break through the imagined linearity of the lived world like a plant through cleared earth. *Hello. You were always there, ahead of us.*

I lived within the perimeter of the Flodden Wall that once encircled the Old Town. Built in response to the Scots' army defeat at the 1513 Battle of Flodden, the wall is almost entirely gone now, but it once reached around the back of the castle and passed along the bottom of my street, where there was a gatehouse called the Netherbow Port, or furthest gateway. This gate was the largest of six, where those who could afford the tax could enter the city. Citizens of the walled city who didn't have the fee to return never left, and the crossroads at the bottom of the street I lived on was known as the world's end. Now that Covid had found us, the famous World's End pub, usually rammed with tourists, had its windows boarded up. It felt like the world's end again. Alexander McCall Smith describes Edinburgh as 'a city of shifting light, of changing skies, of sudden vistas', and it is. Streets become bridges arched over deep canyons; someone steps out from a close you didn't know was there. Spring arrives and overburdens the cherry trees outside of the Canongate Kirk. Winter lifts the roof off the world and doubles the sky's blue. At that moment, the city was suddenly empty and seemed to be unfolding into its own history.

I quelled fear by walking and by noticing: the dates on heavy stone lintels above doors, and the creatures in stone relief emerging out of walls and over windows – how they appeared now there was time to meet them. The way a single body walking down the Royal Mile looked to be threading their way through history – how it opened and closed around them like long grass. As I walked into Edinburgh's rising history, I began to have thoughts about my own: my recent past and further back, to where I come from. Aotearoa. Scotland. I stood in my kitchen, one shaking hand against the window, spanning tenement chimneys and the Salisbury Crags. I was pressed hard against the reality of some big, later-life decisions, and I was thinking that perhaps I should go home.

Home

I was born into the milky light of 1959 New Zealand, the third of four children. We lived in Pukerua Bay, on the west coast of the lower North Island, Te Ika-a-Māui, on the shore of the Tasman Sea, Te Tai-o-Rehua (although we only knew the English names back then). My parents' story is a love story. They swam every day of summer, the two of them making their way to the beach down the goat track opposite our house, towels slung over their shoulders. They never, to my knowledge, got bored with each other. Mum was one of those people who woke up feeling optimistic, flinging open curtains and planning the meals for the day. She loved to produce themed dinner parties, which were attended by their friends and, when we were old enough, ours. Dad was a piano tuner and self-taught musician. He played with jazz bands in Wellington well into his 80s and, playing his accordion, performed for most cultural groups or clubs in the city.

We kids knew our place by heart and skin and breath and salty limbs. We balanced on logs in thumping surf on winter days; turned wet, gritty jeans away from chafed ankles with stinging hands. In the bodily way of children, we knew where we were from. We were from the beach down the hill from our house. This is part of what home in Aotearoa New Zealand still means to me, and this elemental sense of belonging was part of what I longed for in that fearful time when Covid arrived. But really what I was missing doesn't exist as a place, it is a thing that happens, a wild coexistence of self and world, and it happens most readily to and through children.

My son, Elliot, was born in Taranaki in the auspicious year of 1984. Six years later, my non-binary kid, Tamara, was born in Wellington. Tamara's father, Bennett, was a Jewish man from South Africa, who came to New Zealand in his 20s to leave behind the apartheid system. As children, Bennett's parents and their families had fled to South Africa from Latvia, escaping persecution. Elliot's father, Kester, was the New Zealand-born son of post-war English immigrants from an aristocratic line, so Elliot's name is listed in *Burke's Peerage*. I feel a bit awkward including this link to the aristocracy, but it's part of the story. Tamara is an artist and a ranger. Elliot runs a small wildlife ecology business in South Brisbane. When I walk in the bush with my kids – in Australia or New Zealand – they might stop by a tree or a fern and name it, sometimes in its layers: indigenous, local, Latin, and this can feel a little like walking into a poem, which can feel a little like walking into a place.

I was born at the centre of the world, but so is every child. The word 'Home' is so promising and beautiful: the two pillars of the H held upright by its strong cross-beam, and the 'ome' a kind of chant word, and all of it so beautifully arranged, as if with spirit levels and all the other tools for keeping things true. Yet, as an adult, I have felt no story of belonging, not one that I could properly tell and wear. I have lived my life on peripheries, mostly circling small, known places, being a single parent, a writer, a student, a creative writing teacher, until in 2016 I moved to Scotland and felt parts come together in a way that suggested I belonged. Belonged, until the day I wanted to go home.

Suitcases

It was March 2020, the beginning of the first lockdown across the UK. I had recently given my friend Pier a key to my flat, which felt like a small but important security. Like me, Pier lived, still lives, in a tenement building in the centre of the Old Town of Edinburgh. His flat was about two streets away from mine, but we both lived on hills, so we could see each other's buildings. A few days into lockdown, Pier told me that he wanted me to know exactly where his flat was, and he devised a plan to wave an Argentine flag (he was born in Argentina) out of his window at a specified time. At 9.30am, as agreed, I looked out beyond the rows of chimney pots and sloping slate roofs, between the tall thoughts of an old walled-in Edinburgh, and there it was. A small movement of blue and white with a flicker of yellow from its sun, the Sol de Mayo, the backwards and forwards of the Argentine flag. So then I knew exactly where Pier lived. I could see the street, the tenement, and the long, elegant window with its waving flag.

I met Pier when we worked together as learning advisors at Muirhouse Library in North Edinburgh – in a community damaged by unemployment and poverty. Pier speaks ten languages and has recently been learning Arabic, so maybe 11 now, which meant he could converse with the many immigrant and refugee families who came to the library to fill in forms, to enquire about English classes, and to find community. These families were bringing new shapes and stories to the very place-specific disenfranchised howl that seemed to haunt Muirhouse – the howl that comes when so many of your own stories have been erased. Working with Pier in that challenging environment, I learned that I could trust him. When the Covid deaths grew and ambulances wailed in the empty streets, and I suddenly wanted to go back to

New Zealand, I knew I could ask him to pick up the trailing ends of my abrupt exit.

Pier came to my flat. We didn't hug, although seeing a person in the flesh was so comforting. Pier said, *Find out if you can sublet. Don't let this beautiful flat go, Lynn, before you know what you are doing.* I showed him the pile I had made of things he might want. We stood (I admit) side by side and looked out of my kitchen window to his window across the way. We didn't hug when he left. I put things into rubbish bags to throw out. Clothes and bits and pieces I didn't want anyone to have to sift through. I carried them down the 70 steps to the bins beside my building. I climbed the steps again and washed and washed my hands. I made a pile of stuff to go to charity shops when or if they opened again. I guiltily took a pot plant down to the shared courtyard and left it there. I climbed the 70 steps again and washed and washed my hands. I spoke to my kids in Wellington and Brisbane. I cancelled my organic box. I cancelled my hard-to-get grocery order from Tesco. I topped up my gas and electricity cards to cover a month. I didn't know if I'd be back so didn't say anything to my landlord. I emptied the fridge and put the contents in rubbish bags and made more trips down to the bins. I climbed up the 70 steps and washed and washed my hands. I took photos of all the books on my bookcase and other things in my flat so I would remember what was there.

I was anxious. I knew things could go wrong. A few days before, a flight I had booked had disappeared. I'd gone online, with a horrible presentiment, to check my flight only to see that the first of its three parts, Edinburgh to London, was gone. Nobody had contacted me or followed up. It was just gone. An unfamiliar terror landed. I phoned my travel agent and she tried to pull the flight up on her computer, but by then the whole thing had disappeared. I asked her if there were other flights to

New Zealand, and she said no. I put the phone down, shaking and empty-headed except for herring-gulls of fear flapping and screeching. I phoned another travel agent and found a man, Julian, who promised to get me home. He booked a flight for the early hours of the 25th of March. It transited through America and at this point in the Covid crisis you could only transfer through America if you had an ESTA, an entry visa I'd had to get for a holiday with my kids in America just weeks before. I paid the incredibly inflated price for the ticket. I was allowed to take two suitcases.

Later that night I had an email saying something about ESTAs being revoked. I emailed Julian who said, *It's okay. You have the paperwork that says you can go through.* I slept, badly. At 3.30am I was dragging two suitcases, one by one, down 70 steps to catch a taxi to the airport. There was a small group of young people on the street, doing what young people do, thinking they will live forever. The taxi driver was nice. It was, in a weird way, fun to be leaving the neighbourhood; it had been a while. I saw that the daffodils were out.

There was nowhere to get food at the airport except for a dispenser for sweets, crisps and soft drinks. Some people were social distancing, others not so much. I lined up to check in, but part-way through the process the check-in officer's face fell. She told me my ESTA had been revoked. All ESTAs had been revoked at midnight. We both stood there for a while. She asked someone else to look at her computer, and that person saw the same thing. I dragged my two suitcases to some empty chairs, sat down and phoned Julian. He promised he would find another flight. He'd do whatever it took to get me home. I waited. He found me a flight that was leaving in about five hours, this time through Kuala Lumpur and Sydney. One suitcase. I got a taxi back to my flat, dragged my suitcases, one by one, up 70 steps and downsized to one suitcase. I found some non-perishable snacks still lurking in my cupboards and phoned for another taxi. It was the same taxi driver who had taken me the first time. When he dropped me off, he said, kindly, 'I hope I dinnae see you again.' I got in line to check-in. Someone behind me was talking on her phone and standing too close. There were not many people, though. There were not many flights. I got to the check-in officer, and she looked at my ticket. She told me I couldn't get on that flight because borders in both Malaysia and Australia were closing as we spoke. She couldn't allow me to get on the plane. I might get all the way to Sydney and be sent back. I took my suitcase back to the empty seats and phoned Julian. He said she's wrong. He sent me a picture of some site saying the borders were still open. He asked to speak to the check-in officer.

I lined up for check-in maybe six times. The check-in officer wouldn't speak to Julian. Her information and orders came from Head Office in London. I did all sorts of things I never usually do. Made a nuisance of myself. Cried in public. Acted in a way that made people look at me. Tried to force the check-in officer to speak to Julian. Persisted when I should have stopped. I said, *Let me get into Sydney, my son will drive from Brisbane to pick me up.* That wasn't the point. We both knew that. She got cross. She said my travel agent just didn't want to lose his sale. This bit of information stuck. Yes, I thought. He doesn't want to lose his sale. His incredibly expensive one-way ticket. I apologised to the long-suffering check-in officer and dragged my suitcase to the empty seats. And then a kind of peace fell on me, and fall it did: over my head, along my arms, down my sides, and it landed in my feet. I'm not going to get home, I thought. And that's okay. Just go home. To that other home. I phoned Julian one last time. He talked about a flight going through . . . I don't remember now . . . early the next morning, and I said no. And my kids said no. It was too dangerous now. I couldn't go home.

I walked to the airport taxi stand, dragging my one suitcase. The taxi drivers flocked around me asking if I was off the Heathrow flight, was the Heathrow flight in? I didn't think so. Although the state I was in, it might have been, and I didn't see it. *We've been here eight hours with no customers*, they said to me. *Eight hours!* I don't care, I thought. I just want to go home. I stumbled into a taxi and gave my address again. I sat back against the seat and looked out of the window. I thought of the piles of stuff at my flat, scattered and unlovely. I thought for one breath-catching moment that it wasn't a home, it was just a patched-together thing, it had been so easily taken apart: binned, spread across the floor or piled in a corner for someone to pick up. Then I remembered dismantling my parents' home, and how that warm, valuable, solid home, that anchor for me and for my children, turned into piles of stuff, some of which you couldn't give away. And how, as that sad day unfolded, it felt like what was precious and memorable about my parents' lives was dissolving in my hands. And then I thought again about my flat, that I'd have to put everything back, but I'd do it slowly, and I'd reassign value to every little thing, I'd re-make home.

My friends in Edinburgh were going to ground. We literally couldn't look after each other, but also most of them had families to care for. And to be honest, I'm not good at asking for help. So, there was aloneness. And silence – in my flat, on the street, in the park, an uncanny silence. No plane tracked across the sky. The sky grew and grew and grew. We quiet walkers of the Old Town began to feel our size, as humans. We were small. I longed for my kids. I devised a new, soon to be horribly familiar, military-style way of doing things, to stay safe. The steps leading up to and following a walk were many. I had a 'contamination zone', a set of shelves just inside the door for walking paraphernalia: scarves, jacket, gloves, masks, a spritzer of water and bleach. There was the shopping delivery hunt – booking a grocery order for a month ahead. There was the growing fear of other people, and their fear of me. But then, when I became more used to the fear and exhaustion, another feeling drifted up from a different part of myself; it was a feeling of relief to still be in Scotland. The fight-or-flight response had eased, and I began to think and feel in a more integrated way. I lifted my head and looked around, and I remembered my love for a place that had put its arms around me.

When I reassembled my flat – returning everything to its drawer, its shelf, its cupboard, its hook – it was as though I were applying that sticky membrane to the inside of an eggshell. Not nest-building, with its connotations of ingress and egress, of gathering and chattering. No, I was building an egg that I could hunker in while I saw the virus out, and still be in Scotland when I emerged.

It was this many-sided unresolved self, with its pulls between countries and beloveds and hard-won freedoms, that stood in the reassembled flat and thought, What now, and felt (invoked, conjured) a shake in the atmosphere and she was there, my Scottish grandmother's younger sister, Vida. Mad, bad, and dangerous to know, but I had always wanted to know her. I felt her presence. Did I feel the fabric of her jacket and her shirt? It was as though she passed through me into my living room. For a fleeting moment I hoped she was there as a kind of spirit guide through the pandemic, but she wouldn't have it. She just said, *Here we are, two misunderstood self-exiles. Ha! You could put the record straight, you know.* And then, in my imagination (because I couldn't actually see her), she perched on the edge of my pink charity-shop couch and lit a cigarette.

From the little information I had, I knew that Vida's life had been perilous and difficult. This knowledge was a strange sort of comfort in that moment when history was lifting to the surface. In the silence of my flat I told myself that I would unpack Vida's life. I'd write her back into family history, because why should she be left out?

Vida

> I am caught in the hinge of a slowly opening door, between one age and another. Between the tradition of respectability . . . and the new age.
> —Robin Hyde, *A Home in This World*

I got the story of Vida, in fragments, from my grandmother Nen, her sister. Some parts told directly to me and my siblings, and other parts for adult ears only, but overheard: *violence, divorce, the street*. This shadowy story landed very deeply in me. I was the middle daughter, the quiet one, feeling my way around the edges of things – school, words, my own shape. Did I have a shape of my own? I was interested in this woman from my family who didn't toe the line. Hers seemed to me to be a story of youth and the making of sometimes terrible, sometimes liberating choices. I listened and salted away each scrap. The way my grandmother talked about Vida stays with me too. I didn't hear judgement, there was no holier-than-thou tone. I heard a sister talking about her sister, to keep her alive. Over the years I tried, in different settings, with different relatives, to find more of the pieces. When I was 19, I spent four months travelling on my own in Europe, at one point visiting my Great-Uncle Jim in Banchory, Aberdeenshire. Jim was my grandmother's eldest brother. By then an elder of the Kirk (*Tell your grandmother that, it will give her a laugh*), Jim discouraged me from visiting Vida and clearly didn't want to talk about her. I wish I had asked more about her, that I hadn't taken my cue so obediently and closed the conversation. I wish I had looked for her.

I started properly looking for her decades later, in my little flat, in an emptied-out Edinburgh. I was looking for her, but also she was standing behind me watching me look. She was company as she arrived in scraps from Ancestry.com: a name, a date, a photograph. I found Ancestry.com both compelling and a bit soul-sickening. It was like being addicted to Facebook, where you look and look to see what's going on, when the question of what is going on might be best directed back to yourself. Either way, I couldn't stop looking. I'm not a genealogist and I wasn't that interested in building a huge family tree, or in making a diorama for family members to move around in. So, what was I doing? I was calling to her. To Vida. But it was tiring work pulling the past into the present. You can't pull up one person without pulling up others, and soon the floor was covered with the 'profiles' of kin who were strangers. I found generations and generations of Aberdeenshire farmers. What should I do with them? One day, on my walk down the Royal Mile to Holyrood Park, I felt like I was carrying something heavy. When I got to the park, I climbed to where I could look out to sea, right across the Firth of Forth to North Berwick and the lighthouse on Bass Rock, then I sat beside a rowan tree on a slope of grass in soft rain to put it down, that weight, to feel a soft, wet breeze drift across my face, my hair, my hands.

*

Her full name was Vida Ann Ruxton Johnston until she married and then it was Gray. Which feels like a sleight of hand. Vida's husband, Henry Gray, was a well-off older man who went to 'the club' and who was violent to her. She left him, which was radical for those days. And she spent some time in a psychiatric institution, but I don't know when or where or for how long. I do know, from earlier research for a Women's Studies paper on women in New Zealand psychiatric institutions, that in the early-to-mid 20th century, women were committed for being 'different', for not wanting to be a wife, for not doing the housework, for getting postpartum psychosis or depression. And often they weren't released until a relative claimed them. I had read two such files from Porirua Psychiatric Hospital, at the Porirua Hospital Museum when the woman who said I couldn't read the files pointedly left two of them open on her desk when she went out to get us tea. I don't need to tell you. They would make you weep. I thought about women waiting for a family member to release them. I imagine the laws at the heart of the British empire would have been similar to the laws in its farthest outpost. I knew so little about Vida, scraps enough to make a doll's quilt, not enough to cover a person.

I ordered a marriage certificate from National Records of Scotland. Vida married 29-year-old Henry Clarihew Gray on the 4th of June 1928, on her 19th birthday. Henry was an ironmonger, a business he inherited from his father. They were married in St Machar, Aberdeenshire, and their son, Henry Douglas (Doug), was born a year later. I kept looking and found evidence of a divorce, so I paid for another certificate. Vida and Henry divorced in 1941 after 12 years of marriage. Did Vida leave Henry because he was violent? Did Henry divorce Vida because she was mad? Who is the most unhinged in an impossible relationship can be a moot point. I found a copy of Henry Gray's death certificate (If this is wrong of me, I thought, Too late, I'm in too deep). Henry died of alcoholic cirrhosis of the liver aged 69. On the certificate, Vida is named as his wife. I kept looking and found that five years after their divorce, Vida and Henry remarried. How did this divorce and then remarriage go down in 1940s Aberdeen? And what did Vida do in those five unmarried years?

Ancestry.com said Doug is their only child, but I had a hunch there were more. You're reliant on the accuracy of the scribe unless there are official documents to back up the information. Ancestry.com feels to me like a kind of ballad (although not lovely) where the stories of families and communities change shape a little in each singer's mouth. I didn't know that Vida had a child. I had never heard about him.

I listened back, trying to remember more of my grandmother's stories about Vida, and didn't hear anything new, but this memory came: one time when I was maybe ten, and we were visiting her house in Otūmoetai, Tauranga, my grandmother drank so much gin my parents had to put her to bed. I can see her armchair, back-on to me as I stand in the doorway, and my parents on either side of her, and my usually graceful grandmother stumbling. I didn't know then about those days when persevering tips into falling down. I didn't put reasons around it. I just watched, bewildered, and embarrassed for her.

I spent most of the hours of each day on Ancestry.com, Scotland's People, Papers Past, Find a Grave. I pored over old passenger lists (so much of my family's story is embedded in passenger lists). I spread questions and fragments across the living room floor. I knelt over them until my legs and back and arms were sore. I made notes and began the first of many visual pictures, showing myself what I had found. I was conjuring up the dead. We were playing hide and seek. As I looked another memory came of my father telling me once that he didn't much like John Johnston, his grandfather, Vida's father. And across his face when he said this went one of those expressions that are deep and a bit unfathomable. I think parts of family history are passed on in this way, through a wash of expression, like a wave. Unless you're quick it's impossible to find out where it came from. By the time the wave has washed up on the shore of a certain face, who can know how far back it started? Certainly, this expression had crossed the world.

My sleep was even more broken than usual. My head full of unfinished stories. When I did sleep, I woke suddenly with a frightened feeling and my throat slightly raw, as though I'd been doing that breath-screaming that sometimes happens in and because of nightmares. It felt to me as though she, Vida, had changed her mind, she'd had enough, and was telling me to stop unearthing old stories. Not to stir up family trouble. To leave (un)well enough alone. I lay back on my bed, my heart thumping, my vision pulsing. I wondered if my slightly sore throat was the beginning of the virus.

I did a family constellations session once. This is a therapeutic system performed in a group where, under the guidance of a therapist, a particular family relationship is explored within the context of the 'constellation' of your family, so that possibly unrecognised dynamics or 'systemic entanglements' that span generations might show themselves. These entanglements are described by one of the founders of family therapy, Hungarian American psychiatrist Iván Böszörményi-Nagy as 'invisible loyalties'. People in the group stand in for family members, as you do for them when it's their constellation. I found it an eerie experience; you become inhabited by the person you're standing in for in a way I didn't expect. During my constellation, the woman who stood in for Nen had her back to the goings-on of the rest of the family and was looking towards Scotland. Longing to be there. *It was so green*, the woman who 'was' my grandmother said. And she wanted to return. She wanted to go back.

One day I found a passenger list which told me that in 1926 my family travelled from Aberdeen to Auckland. On board were Helen, my great-grandmother, 16-year-old Vida, her brothers Stuart and Douglas and her older sister Nen, and Nen's husband Jim Davidson (my grandparents). The final passenger was my grandparents' one-year-old son, John. The two siblings not on the boat were Vida's eldest brother, who was staying in Scotland, and her next-eldest brother, who was already in New Zealand.

When my family arrived to an Auckland autumn, they had been at sea for 42 days. I imagine them standing at the rails of the *Remuera* with their good coats on, looking a bit peely-wally and scanning the wharf for my great-grandfather, John Johnston, who had travelled out to New Zealand eight months previously. I imagine my great-grandfather hugging his family – if a Protestant Scot would do such a thing – and holding his grandson. The family together again.

My great-grandfather had been intending to buy a farm in the South Island. Farming in Scotland was in decline, and New Zealand in the early 20s was doing well, thanks to a dairying boom. But the depression he hoped to leave behind in Britain followed him, and by 1926 prices for New Zealand agricultural products were plummeting, and mass unemployment was on the horizon. By the time his family were part-way through their voyage, something in him had shifted, some certainty was undoing itself. I imagine him, my great-grandfather, at the wharf in Auckland, organising the transfer of bags, ordering a taxi, and in something about his head-down busyness, his family slowly picking up that all was not as it should be.

Only four months after they arrived, my great-grandparents and their two youngest children, Vida and Douglas, boarded a ship to return to Scotland, leaving family and the dream of a farm in New Zealand behind. My great-grandfather, who was once head of a family farm in Aberdeenshire, would go back to running pubs and farming leased land to make a living. I can imagine that return sea journey, in steerage, in the confines of shared bunkrooms without privacy or comfort, being a cruel sort of hiatus when you are thinking about leaving behind a grandson, sons and a daughter, a sister, a nephew, brothers, and the hope for a better life. Within two years the youngest sibling, Douglas, would return to New Zealand to live with my grandparents and their two young sons at 39 Derwent Street,

Island Bay on Wellington's wild south coast. But this wasn't the end of my family's migrations and reverse migrations. As the two world wars created urgencies for a safer, more prosperous life, some of my family moved between hemispheres with children and furniture and that unsettling, sometimes humiliating thing called hope.

Vida didn't seem to suffer from the sort of hope that has you moving across the world. She never returned to New Zealand after that first journey with her parents. So, what were her visions for the future in troubled times? The only photos I have of Vida are of a young woman. I have held her there, in youth, and championed her from there. She, marrying at 19 (in a bid for freedom from a grim, exacting father?), and me at 19 leaving New Zealand for Europe, also after a kind of freedom, something different and particular and my own. I want so much to see the shape of Vida's life. If marriage didn't work, did she find something else that did? What were her lowest points and how did she climb out of them? I contacted a woman at NHS Grampian Archives who said she would look to see if and when Vida was in a psychiatric institution. She said that Vida's unusual name would make her easy to find. But lockdown meant she couldn't access the records, and just as it looked like they might finally get back into the building, some football players breached lockdown conditions causing a spike in Covid cases in Aberdeen so it was all put off again. That night, I listened to the news as I made dinner and heard that the pub the footballers went to was the Adam Lounge & Hawthorn Bar. The Hawthorn Bar is the name of one of the Aberdeen pubs my great-grandfather owned. I stabbed at the carrots and onions; I'd have to wait a bit longer to find out. I chopped and chopped until all I could make was soup. I left it simmering. I looked at Vida's photo, the in-profile photo of a beautiful young woman with a wavy, fashionable bob, wearing a dark-coloured velvet jacket with thin satin ribbon edging the collar. She looked intelligent, focused, gentle and determined. She looked like a woman moving into a new era. She looked as sane as the sun, if a little sad.

I found a gravestone for Henry Gray. Henry's parents are named, and Henry and Vida's son Doug is named. There is no mention of Vida. And as I looked at it, I thought how that's not good enough. It's not good enough when women are curated out. When mothers are curated out: *Too difficult, too mad, too wrong-headed, too inconvenient.* I rifled through the papers on the floor, found Vida's birth certificate and stuck it on the wall above my desk, because once upon a time a little girl was born.

She was born where Macbeth died

My great-grandfather owned the Lumphanan Hotel, a late 19th-century pub that is now known as the Macbeth Arms. It was then and is now the only hotel in the tiny rural Aberdeenshire village of Lumphanan and is where Vida and her younger brother Douglas were born. On Vida's birth certificate the home address is simply 'the Hotel'.

Lumphanan is famous for the 1057 Battle of Lumphanan between Mac Bethad mac Findláich – in English, Macbeth, – and Máel Coluim mac Donnchada, the future King Malcom III; the battle where Macbeth was killed. There are three main sites connected with Macbeth in Lumphanan. There is Macbeth's Well, where he drank before the battle, a stone-lined well built into a bank and which emerges from foliage like a heavily browed face. Then there is the Macbeth Stone, a large stone in a field where, it is said, Macbeth was beheaded. And to the north of the village, on Perk Hill, is the cairn that shows where Macbeth was buried before being disinterred, to be re-buried on the Isle of Iona, the traditional burial place of kings. A stone-lined well, a stone, a cairn. I want to reach through the computer and touch those three stony memorials. I haven't been to the historic memorials for Macbeth in Lumphanan, but I have been to Dunkeld along the River Tay to visit the remaining ancient oak of *Macbeth*'s Birnam Wood: a giant with one of its limbs propped by a human-made crutch, and who seems about to move again, albeit slow and lurching.

I have always been drawn to the Scottish play. The terrible, powerful love between Macbeth and Lady Macbeth, and that dark glimmer of our worst most derailed ambitious selves. But there are two Macbeths – the invented and the real – and they are very different men. While both were skilled warriors, the real 11th-century Scottish King was a ruddy, fair-haired man, not the brooding dark-haired Macbeth of the play. The real Macbeth was respected by his people and ran an efficient government and as one of the last Gaelic kings, if he had lived, would have been a better king for Scotland. I read about this Macbeth in Scottish writer and historian Fiona Watson's 2010 book, *Macbeth: A True Story*, a book I found at Waterstones on Princes Street, but discovered was written, in first draft at least, at Watson's friend's house in Christchurch, New Zealand. Watson writes in the introduction that 'In these pages you will find a very real king presiding over a sophisticated, vital kingdom which, though situated on the margins of Europe, was still part of a dynamic Continental society.' Shakespeare's Macbeth, on the other hand, Watson writes, was inherently tribal and violent, upholding the 'Noble Celt' mythology whose flip side was 'Barbarian'.

Macbeth is set in the 11th century but was written in 1606; its first performance was in the royal court of King James I (of England and Ireland) and VI (of Scotland), who was patron of Shakespeare's theatre company, the King's Men. Shakespeare had King James in mind when he wrote *Macbeth*. Its shadows reflect the paranoia of the Reformation. Shakespeare's Macbeth also portrays a growing perception of the bloody and brutal Highlander. King James's attempts to defuse the powerful clan system in Scotland (and their limited submission to his rule) were framed as 'bringing civilisation' to the Gaelic-speaking Highlands and Islands of Scotland. This included suppression of language and culture, the taking of land and the fracture of families where, Watson writes, eldest children of clan chiefs were removed from their family and home and taken to mainland schools where they would get a 'civilised education in English'.

Shakespeare's play about ambition gone haywire may present a Macbeth very different from the real king, but, as Watson says, 'this is not the English playwright's fault, since he was merely repeating, with some of his own embellishment, what was already being said about Macbeth by the Scots themselves'. Watson writes that the political powerbase had shifted from the Highlands and the clan system to southern Scotland, and there was a tide of anti-Celtic feeling from both within and outwith Scotland, and Macbeth had 'been transformed from a beloved father of his people into a bloody tyrant'.

Macbeth was written during the return of the plague in London – with the fearful and strange beliefs that such events evoke. We want, don't we, in moments of such upheaval in state and world affairs, for things to hold still, for something 'other' (however weird) to be causing the unrest? The play, seemingly awash in supernatural influences, takes the temperature of its world – you could say it reads the room. The story of the hitherto fairly unknown Scottish king who died five hundred years before (in Lumphanan, not Dunsinane) begins and ends with witches, reflecting a time when the persecution of 'witches' is being given fuel by King James and his fevered treatise, *Daemonologie*; a persecution which will go on in Europe for the next three hundred years, and which, in the truly terrible shapeshifting properties of the oppression and persecution of women, carries on still.

Vida walks past Macbeth's Well on her way to school.

 Her hands dip into its ion-stippled space

 for the smirr of earthy mist

 from the constant spring

Its heavily browed stone face frightens her, but she can't resist it. My grandmother's hand tugs her away from the well, back onto the road. My grandmother, Vida's big sister, the eldest girl, charged with caring when that wasn't her disposition. Nor was not-caring. There were just other things she wanted. She had other ambitions.

    Little Vida wipes her damp hand across her face

*

On summer evenings I walked up to Edinburgh Castle, just a quick walk from my flat. The face of the castle was washed with a white night-time light. We socially distanced, masked residents of Edinburgh wandered around the forecourt, stood on the drawbridge, or rested against a pillar atop which a man on a horse held something aloft. At one side of the forecourt, you looked across the Old Town towards the Pentland Hills. At the other, you looked across Princes Street Gardens to the New Town – all strangely empty, yet suddenly full of their own shapes and layered histories.

My vision seemed acute on those long, quiet nights: *Here is the rough rock the castle stands on, and there is the dent of a desire line across a faraway hillside, and see, a hundred feet below, that twist of ivy growing around the metal railing on the steep black steps.* It was magical, and vertiginous. Sometimes kids in a car made a couple of quick noisy circles of the forecourt and then drove off, having broken the spell of space and silence. At other times we were all at once still, and there was only the sound of breath against fabric, and everything was strange and frightening and beautiful.

One night when I went up to the castle, I saw a young woman with long red hair reach through the sash window of her flat that is on the top floor of a medieval tenement, as if to feed birds. I stood there looking at her: her hair, her arms, the gesture, and behind me, the castle. I couldn't but be in a fairy tale. Then I went on to the small, hidden plaque tucked against a building at the top of the Royal Mile commemorating the women burned as witches on the forecourt. I traced my finger over a bronze serpent, cupped hands, flowers, and a tiny bowl for water. A small, muddled monument that doesn't know what its job is, unlike the elevated statues edging the forecourt, that do. As we walked around on these light summertime nights, wearing our masks, it felt to me as though we had a story to tell but were telling it without speaking. The story was about a global plague that causes all of the other stories to lie down along the line of their own shadows, some of them losing their gloss and their shape. We walked around in the bright darkness, bewildered, breathing into the fragile protection of cotton and paper.

One day I will visit the Lumphanan of Vida's birth. I will stay at the Macbeth Arms where she was born, and when I head out to climb Perk Hill to reach Macbeth's cairn, I will ask Vida to come with me, like a sister. Time moves around us like the planets, and we are stirred together beneath it.

Ambulances drown out the herring gulls

Vida looks over my shoulder at a printout of a great-great-uncle, another farmer, another John Johnston, and sniffs impatiently. She leaves the living room and I hear her tuck herself along the deep sill of the kitchen window, where I like to sit and look out at the crags with their crows and at the tenement chimneys where herring gulls are nesting. She calls me through to look at something.

I stand at the kitchen door. She's pulling on a cigarette and staring out the window. I admire her profile, the rounded cheekbone, the fine nose, my grandmother's profile. She slips off her two-tone brogues and drops them to the floor.

'There's an ambulance outside that tenement,' she says, waving towards it with her cigarette.

'There are ambulances everywhere,' I reply.

'But look, it's right here in our close.' *Our* close. I feel a wash of warmth, of comfort. Still.

'I don't want to look.'

'Just as well some of us don't mind looking,' she replies with some kind of meaningful emphasis. I stand there a moment in case she's going to unpack that enigmatic statement, but she doesn't. I go back to the living room. Why are you even here, I think, but don't say it in case she goes away.

'You could just tell me your story,' I call back, 'save me a lot of trouble.' And Vida laughs.

'How would that work? Taking dictation from a ghost. A spirit.' She laughs again. 'My father was a spirit merchant.'

'I know,' I say, but I don't want to play word association, or be ironic, or joke at all today.

Another ambulance wails. 'It's a bit like the war,' Vida calls through again, 'without the bombs. There's even a field hospital in . . .'

'I know,' I cut her short. 'I know. It's awful.' I am on my knees spreading out centuries of relatives, many of whom had business with a spade and a plough. And then some, perhaps reluctantly, had business with a gun.

Two

Door into the forest

If not now, when

Like my ancestors before me who wanted to better their lives in an era of war and Depression, it was in the context of my own small wars and personal depression that I packed my bags and moved to Scotland, hoping for a better life, a rich third act of my own making.

Some years earlier, in that strange, quiet time when my youngest had left home, I'd asked myself, what now? I had my creative writing teaching work at Whitireia Community Polytechnic, although funding cuts and the pressure to get student 'bums on seats' were making teaching exhausting and unsafe. *I had my teaching work.* My son was studying marine biology and ecology at Victoria University in Wellington, and my younger kid was in the far north doing an environmental management course. *My children were out in the world.* My mother was going ever deeper into Alzheimer's, and my older sister and I were visiting our parents regularly to cook for and generally support them. *I had my parents.*

Sibling relationships were fraying and difficult. We saw things differently and argued. There is nothing unique in our family flailing and fighting at this moment of juggling growing children, empty nests, ailing parents and our own reckoning with advanced middle age. My older sister moved to Melbourne to be near her children and grandchildren, just after my younger sister and her family came home from several years in the UK. I had been reliably at home. I felt the walls closing in. I'd had no breath, no moment, between caring for children and caring for parents. I was still doing my own writing in the spaces of time left to me around the edges of a full-time job and family commitments. It felt urgent to put writing at the front of my life. So, not long after Tamara left home, the idea came to me that I too could allow myself to move. I left my increasingly stressful job in Wellington to live in Nelson and take up a creative writing teaching position at the Nelson Marlborough Institute of Technology. My mother was in a full-time secure care facility by then, and I regularly flew across the Cook Strait (in frighteningly small planes) to see her, my dad, and my kids. In this new place, in this move that I had chosen, space seemed to open. I felt my outline sharpen. Then, only a few months after starting at NMIT, my son's father, my ex-husband, (who had only recently visited us and other friends and family in New Zealand) killed himself. He paddled a canoe into the North Sea from St Ninian's Isle off the Shetland Islands, where he was living, and never came back.

I flew up to Wellington and organised a memorial service for Kester on Pukerua Bay beach, where he and I and my kids had all grown up. Then Elliot flew to Lerwick in Shetland to join his half-brother, Eldon, and Kester's partner for a memorial service there. The service was held in a small stone church. There was a cappella singing, and Kester's favourite canoe sat where the coffin would otherwise be.

I spent as much time as I could with my son and with my parents. Less than a year after I began my job at NMIT, the creative writing programme, including my position, was dramatically cut back following a change of government and some tough funding decisions, and I handed in my notice. I got a scholarship through Massey University, which allowed me to start a PhD looking at poetic repetition both critically in the work of other poets and creatively through a collection of my own poetry. By this time Elliot had finished his degree and was living in Brisbane, and Tamara was about to take up a ranger position for the Department of Conservation in the Ruahine Range, a couple of hours north of Wellington. My mother was very close to dying. My sisters supposed I would return home. I felt unseen, unheard.

I got a job tutoring in creative writing at the University of Melbourne. Some backs turned. I flew to Melbourne to start work and then home for my mother's funeral a few weeks later. It was an awful, lonely time. On the morning I heard that Mum had died, I was standing at the window of the room I was teaching in, looking out at the elegant grounds of the university's Parkville Campus and waiting for the class to start, when a student, a young man, asked me if I was okay. I was grieving, and I was hurt, and not much at that moment was okay, but I looked at him and smiled, saying I was okay even though we both knew different. His kindness got me through that class. After my mother's funeral, I flew back to Melbourne, worked on my PhD, lectured and tutored. I was looking more and more towards Scotland, and in 2013 I was awarded the month-long Hawthornden Literary Retreat at Hawthornden Castle, just outside of Edinburgh. As I flew across the world, excitement kept washing through my body. I seemed to be flying in the right direction. During my time in Scotland, I gave a paper on repetition in Kathleen Jamie's poetry collection *The Tree House* at a contemporary poetry conference held at the University of Manchester. And, sitting on a bench in the grounds of the university, I interviewed Jamie herself for my PhD. When the residency was up, and it was time to fly back to Melbourne, I didn't want to leave Scotland. I had seen some deepening possibilities for my life there, and I couldn't let them go.

In 2016, at the age of 57, with my PhD in my pocket, I answered what was calling me and relocated to Edinburgh. I can say with my hand on my heart that making that decision was terrifying. But the old rabbinical question 'If not now, when' usefully haunted me. I have often not had secure income. I live precariously to say the least. But I made the decision to cross the world partly because I had spent too many hours fighting my corner and needed a new start, and partly because I wanted so much to live in Scotland. *I wanted it.* But this wanting didn't make it an easy decision; it took a lot of counselling hours to let myself do what I wanted to do. And when I did, no skies fell.

I could have made a decisive move towards my own life, my own shape in the world, much earlier, before I had children, as several of my women friends did, to avoid some fractures of identity that can come with raising children close to your family of origin. But, although I can't say it was a choice to stay, there is something undeniably lucky and precious about raising children inside a loving, noisy family, where almost every family event includes three generations sitting down at the table together (at one point my parents, grandparents, brother, both sisters, myself, and our respective families all lived in the small seaside town of Pukerua Bay). Also, it is hard to resist the magnetic force of a powerful family, and my family was powerful. It couldn't fathom that you might want something other than what it offered because what it offered was aesthetically beautiful and involved a very particular, Bohemian-looking sort of freedom. And yet, or perhaps *and so*, my family began to feel like a kind of Silicon Valley company, where everything I might possibly want, but nothing I needed, was available.

Despite blanking Scotland – *Just another piece of dirt* – my father was clannish. He had a vision for his family and, I think, a fear of things outside that vision, things he didn't fully understand or feel comfortable with. I felt that fear each time I left the family, the clamour of freight on the DNA line; most especially clamorous, I suspect, for the clan girls and women. There was a moment when I went to university, the only one in my family of origin to go, and I used the word 'campus' at the dinner table, and Dad mocked it, as though it were elitist and not particularly welcome at our table. My father is tricky to catch; he was both conservative and rebellious, encouraging and at times diminishing. He did what I haven't yet done and explored his own Pacific neighbourhood. He looked after his family and his friends. Like his father before him, and his children and grandchildren after him, he had his own business. If he often talked about the importance of acting independently, of being a kind of one-man band, it was the Scottish network that got him his first job. Grandad knew Charles Begg, an ex-Aberdeenshire man, who gave Dad a job working at Beggs Music Store on Willis Street. It was Charles Begg who taught Dad his piano-tuning trade. I have one of Dad's tuning forks, which when knocked against a hard surface makes a perfect wave pattern, a true note, which you can tune to once the high overtones fade out.

In looking for a partner who might liberate me from paradise, I found men who, while they seemed to have all the autonomy in the world themselves, didn't particularly want that for me. I settled down with controlling men. Did they trick me to draw me in? Or did I trick myself into thinking they were what they were not? Perhaps both. On a deeper level it had to do with self-sabotage, and a subconscious pattern of thinking around what I was, and was not, allowed. My identity was fractured by difficult relationships. My identity was fractured by bewilderment. My identity was fractured because I let it be. I left those relationships and was a single parent. My main ambition for my children has been that they would make their own independent way in the world. That they would flower into themselves, and I'd offer masses of love and keep my hands off as much as possible. I would cheer from the sidelines. Being in a different hemisphere from my grown-up children was the only really hard part of my decision to go to Edinburgh. What made it okay was their encouragement. Their support for the life I needed to live felt like the passing on of a gift. Something I had got right.

Skinner's Close

I got a five-year Ancestry visa, packed two suitcases and boarded a plane for Scotland. I found a room in a Victorian terraced house in Musselburgh, at the eastern border of Edinburgh. The owner of the house was a woman around my age whose partner lived a few doors along. In fact, the row of tall, terraced houses was home to a community of lesbian friends who, when they go to a play or a gig at the local theatre, wander along the street front collecting each other. Sometimes I went with them. It was a lovely place to land.

    I held on for dear life to Scotland. I got a job in the local Tesco stacking shelves (I knew my PhD on poetic repetition would come in handy). To get to Tesco I crossed a Roman bridge with ducks and sometimes otters slipping along the river beneath it. I hated working at Tesco, and I got a sore knee and felt old and limpy and annoyed at myself. This wasn't how I'd imagined things turning out. I worked through Christmas and felt sick at the end of each day about all the stuff I was pulling out of boxes, to stack and re-stack shelves. In my spare moments I walked by the River Esk that flows through Musselburgh and empties into the Firth of Forth at the nearby Fisherrow Harbour. The river filled up in me what Tesco had emptied out. When, early in the new year, I got a job in Edinburgh Libraries, I thought I was saved until I saw where I was to work, and I took a deep breath. I moved into a room in a tenement flat in Portobello, a seaside suburb just a few miles from the city centre. I had a view of a bus terminal and beyond that, the North Sea. I loved my view: the big empty buses rocking into the terminal, and the big North Sea rocking up onto the shore. I watched weather coming in. I caught the bus to work, first to Muirhouse Library and then to Granton.

One day at Granton Library an old man brought a box of knitting stuff to the counter. He wanted the library to have it. It belonged to his wife who had recently died. She was very orderly: buttons in a jar, paired up knitting needles, and almost-finished jumpers and cardigans. The crinkly plastic bags holding the wool. A librarian put the box on the floor and, on her knees, quietly went through it, seeing what the knitting group might finish. The knitting group gathered at a table around tea and biscuits and pulled their own half-finished garments out of tote bags, and a couple of them tucked into the soft bulging bags something that the gone-now local woman had half made, to finish.

After work I would walk along Portobello Beach where oystercatchers and gulls made their long end-of-day calls. I fell in love with the beach, its views across to Fyfe and East Lothian, the low-lying smooth lift and fall of hills. I fell in love with their shape and colour and light, the shape and colour and light I didn't know I had been missing. Sometimes I walked to nearby Newhailes Estate and stood at the edge of a tree-lined field from where I could see across the sea to Bass Rock with its gannet colony and its lighthouse.

I finally shifted into my own flat on the fourth floor of a tenement block in Skinner's Close, off the Royal Mile. It was just a short walk from my flat to Holyrood Park where I could still see Bass Rock, beyond North Berwick. I started going out to North Berwick, a one-hour bus journey, to see the pink-footed geese come and go, to climb the Law, to visit the Seabird Centre, and one day to take a guided boat trip to Bass Rock where thousands of gannets circle and land, and where the guide was a New Zealander – a friend of my kid Tamara – who told us about the kittiwake and unselfconsciously made its call. In lockdown I walked around Holyrood Park most days, and I saw how Bass Rock with its Stevenson lighthouse and its whitewash of gannet shit is lit periodically by the sun.

Bright water

I had places that held me when I first lived in Scotland. One of them was the Scottish Poetry Library in Crichton's Close, one of the many closes off the Royal Mile. Its director at the time was Robyn Marsack, a New Zealander and Glaswegian scholar and writer, a gentle welcomer. When I walked into the woody, sunlit poetry library with its floor to ceiling windows and its deck off the mezzanine floor, it made me think of New Zealand. The building could be little sister to the elegant Central Library in Wellington, although that big sister is closed now, due to a change in seismic performance criteria after the Christchurch and Kaikōura earthquakes.

On my first visit I found *The Hidden Place*, a framed map of Scotland made by artist and poet Thomas A. Clark. Like a little loch, it made a pale blue light amongst the forest of books. On the map, a hundred Scottish place names are replaced by phrases that reveal their original meanings. They include 'loch of the night', 'the field of sighing', 'bright water', 'the talkative one' and 'door of the forest'. 'Kestrel moor' is the name for Musselburgh – situated on the fertile, loamy, eastern edge of Edinburgh, and my first home in Scotland. The sea in the map is an airy light blue, too soft for sky and a shade too pale for Madonna. It's an artist's blue, and not one I can name, but I think it's blown through with white, to make it spacious. The land is white. Place names are a deeper blue. Each name references aspects of mythology, history, geography, industry or religion linked to that piece of land. In polyphonic Scotland, place names could be in Gaelic, Pictish, English, Norse, Latin or Scots, but on this map each name reaches through language for another layer of story: 'old deer', 'bay of the bent grass', 'well of the dead', 'field of wild angelica', 'loch of the outcry', 'the common grazings'. To me this map felt wide, inclusive, a type of conversation.

It was at the Scottish Poetry Library that I was asked by poet Jennifer Williams, then Programme Manager there, if I would like to join a collective of 12 women writers to write in response to, and echoing, the collaborative Feministo Postal Art Event of 1975–77. An exhibition and symposium were to be held at Cooper Gallery in Dundee. The Feministo Postal Art Event was a movement where women artists in the UK made their art at home and then posted it to one another, creating home-based galleries, and eventually holding significant public exhibitions of their work. Our 'posting' was digital, on a shared Google Doc, but it was charged with the energy of those women who had, in the 70s, built their creative community, as they were powered by women before them, and so on.

The women I found myself working with were lovely, smart and talented writers. We were Edinburgh-based, but many, like me, had settled in Scotland from different parts of the world. As we wrote, we noticed how collaboration opened up a new, different sort of freedom and ease in terms of getting words on the page. The poems seemed part of a greater 'making', like a river that started and finished somewhere way behind and way beyond any of us. This is true, of course, of every poem ever written, but writing collaboratively made this truth shine more brightly.

The experience of responding to the Feministo project was so generative, so supportive and so exciting that we wanted to keep going at the end of it. We gave ourselves a name – *12* – and each month one of us posts a poem on our Google Doc and we respond to it in any way we choose (no critiques, no pressure). We have gone on to respond to exhibitions at various galleries, including the Fruitmarket Gallery, the National Galleries of Scotland and the Cample Line Gallery. We are still writing together. We wrote together through lockdowns and through some major reconfiguring of lives. We are currently working on a book project with poems that honour a Scottish woman gardener, Norah Geddes (daughter of the more famous Patrick Geddes), who, among other things, designed the lovely West Port Community Garden tucked into a small, steep cranny in the Old Town, among what was then slum housing. It feels good to be celebrating Norah's work and talents, even though I can't be there for the launch of the book or the festival readings. And it is good to go on meeting my writing community down at the river, in the bright water, beside the common grazings and the door into the forest.

*the castle is definitely haunted

It was early September, six months after Covid had sent us home to our flats and our houses. I walked up to visit my favourite grove of silver birches in Holyrood Park. Exhausted from another broken sleep, I lay on my back in the centre of their circle and looked at the shimmering leaves through half-shut eyes. Here and there the bright green leaves were stained with yellow, as though after the long, strange summer, they were trying to remember a thing called autumn, and properly draw it down. I hauled myself to my feet and before leaving rested my ear against one of the young trees. I had read that when sap and water move up through a tree's inner bark it makes a crackling sound, but I didn't expect to hear anything because I didn't have a stethoscope or headphones or any equipment except for my soft ear pressed to the trunk. But I did hear something. I heard a distinct crackling, popping sound. I was listening to the tree drink. It reminded me a bit of those strange and lovely sounds that new babies make when they suckle.

    Silver birches have a shimmery smooth silver trunk (I always want to say stem, as though the trees were huge flowers), but as they get older, the silver is broken through around the foot of the trunk with rough, fissured dark-brown bark, the sort of bark you might see on a pine tree. From a distance, especially in autumn with their bright leaves, they look like pale candles in rustic holders. Close up, they look like the process of ageing. I wondered what I'd hear if I got on my knees and put my ear to the rough stuff, but I didn't dare. I thought of all the bugs living in the crevices that might climb into me as I listened. I felt that I was like the older part of the birch tree, down with the roots, fissuring, growing wider and more accommodating, and helping to hold a younger self up there – a self who sways and chatters, who gets its water and sap after it moves through me and then, up there with the sun, it pays me back with the nutritious, leafy gift of photosynthesis.

I travelled to Scotland four times: as a 19-year-old looking for my own shape in the world; as a 25-year-old with a husband and toddler to visit friends and relatives and to explore; as a single woman in my 50s for a writing residency in a new, more self-focused phase of life; and soon after that, when I went there to live. I went to Scotland, surprisingly, to meet up with my 19-year-old self because it seemed she knew something. In Scotland, for me, time doesn't feel linear. My youth often crosses paths with me. Or lifts up through me like a heron off a loch.

I climbed down the slope from the birches and cut across towards Hunter's Bog to avoid the joggers with their unmasked faces and laboured breathing. Back in my flat I pulled out my diary from that first trip to Scotland. I found a rose pressed at its centre.

It was 1978. I had taken a train from London to Aberdeen and then a bus to Banchory. At 9pm I was sitting in a Banchory bus stop with my backpack resting against my leg, looking out into the dark, not sure how to get to my Great-Uncle Jim's place, when a girl my own age stopped to ask if I was okay. As luck would have it, Liz was a New Zealander on her OE. She told me she was a nurse at Glen O' Dee Hospital, and I could stay at her place for the night if I was stuck, which I was. She sneaked me into the nurses' quarters and made tea and mousetraps, and we talked about New Zealand. She was proud to have bread that was very like New Zealand's favourite Vogel's bread, so I had to be pleased and eat it, even though it had a bit of mould on one of its edges. She showed me photos of a trip she'd taken to Russia; we spread them on the floor around us. At about midnight I crashed in Liz's bed. The next morning, I found my great-uncle and -aunt's place, and they welcomed me into their home, a relative come back from New Zealand. At this time, three of my Great-Uncle Jim's siblings were living in New Zealand, including my grandmother, and one was in Scotland. The one in Scotland was Vida, the relative I most wanted to meet. The one that Uncle Jim didn't want to talk about.

I had just spent four extraordinary months in Europe, most recently in Germany and then Turkey where I had fallen in love with Turkish food, with the late-night cafés, and with the beautiful, repetitious call to prayer. I had also had an affair with a much older man. Germany and Turkey had been marvellous and complicated. After disentangling myself from the affair, I flew out of Germany into England and caught a train to Aberdeen. I was escaping, and nothing much was on my mind but that; I didn't realise that I was travelling towards something. At some point, when the train had crossed into Scotland, I looked out of the window and felt a surprising bolt of recognition. I was 19, and I was not on a quest to locate my ancestry. Far from it. But although I'd never been there before, I knew the place. I knew the shape of the hills, I knew the light, I knew the colours. Still, I was young and distracted. While my body arrived, my head was somewhere else. Here's the dairy entry for my first full day in Scotland:

September, Banchory, cold and windy
I slept late and got a huge breakfast in bed. They have a Canadian couple staying as Aunty Nan does bed and breakfast in the summer. First day of autumn today! Went to see Craigievar Castle (postcard) with Uncle Jim. Very impressed. It is a simple but very beautiful castle with tartan curtains and seat covers. The castle is still being used. Went through what looked like the panel of a wall into a secret windy stone staircase. I think it is the nicest

pay castle I have seen yet. Then we went to Lumphanan and had afternoon tea at my great-grandfather's old hotel, now called the Macbeth Arms. Saw the land my great-grandfather used to own. Saw the church where Nana used to go to Sunday school and saw the mountains with the heather, not in full bloom but you could still see it. I really feel like I have a heritage here – more so than I thought I would before I arrived. Saw some photos of Nana and co. Really tired, went to bed.
*the castle is definitely haunted

Not exactly riveting stuff, and it is childish in tone compared to earlier diary entries with their much more tangled moments.

I turned back to the beginning of my diary, before Germany and Turkey and Scotland. I turned back to my initial arrival into London, where I strained the goodwill of a friend of the family after she kindly invited me to stay at her home in Kent. A few days after I arrived, her son, Simon, came to visit for tea, which, as it was spring, we had in the garden, sitting under a large oak. I thought I was in a Somerset Maugham novel. Simon seemed to find me appealing and started taking me out in his car. We took a trip to Canterbury, and he showed me his old school, in the grounds of Canterbury Cathedral, which my diary records this way:

We went to Simon's old school, an enormous posh private school called 'Kings'. Somerset Maugham went there. He also had his ashes scattered there. Of course the classrooms and 'houses' etc were all enormous old stone places with velvet green lawns and boys walking around in stiff pokey-up white collars and tie, black jackets and stripy trousers. When they go out they wear straw boaters.

In my passive way, I allowed Simon to take me to antique car shows, to his friend John's flat in Holland Park, and to beautiful old pubs in the countryside. His mother began taking me to travel agencies to help organise my next big adventure. In my diary I think this is because she's regretting the few days of being annoyed with me (I rightly surmise this has something to do with Simon) and has decided to make up for it by being helpful. But clearly she wanted me gone. A 19-year-old New Zealander who has never heard of King's Canterbury isn't who she has in mind for her son. I think of Simon – a charming, slightly plump, fair-haired man with good manners who thought I was diverting and a bit odd, in a funny way. I don't think his mother had anything to worry about.

As I write 'In my passive way' I think, But I wasn't passive. I had left behind friends, over-protective parents, siblings, a job in the Advertising Features Department of Press House, and the country I knew, to travel alone in Europe. But when I got there, I had few plans. I failed to think ahead. Part of it was being 19, but part was, is, me. I feel my way forward, almost like a cat does with its long whiskers letting it know if a shape is big enough to step through. Which isn't sensible, and probably stems from some kind of disbelief in my ability to first throw the shape and then step into it. Or the belief that there is a next thing that will hold me.

When I went back to my first travel diary I was amazed at the bravery of my teenage self, her awareness of her sexual power, and how bold she could be. I was quite good at being a teenager, I thought, with some surprise. And yet, something was holding me back. On the one hand, I was wandering around Soho being offered a job in a hippy clothes shop and wondering if I should take it, or getting a lift with people I didn't know from London to the Lake District, or having inadvisable encounters. All of that ordinary experimental young-person stuff. On the other hand, I was writing home to my parents and family enquiring about everyone in my extended family and their goings on as if I were their mother. I even urged my parents to be careful when they were embarking on a cruise to Rarotonga! What was I doing, playing this slightly sticky solicitous role. I bought presents for everyone, including books, which weighed down my backpack, making 'going home' an actual weight on my back almost from the beginning of my journey.

After leaving London, I eventually wound up in Munich, to stay with a Munich-based English couple, Emma and Pete. Another connection through family friends. I slept on the couch in their compact, post-Second World War apartment with its small orange balcony in a street of similar apartment buildings. I liked the utilitarian apartment block with its tiny balconies, I liked the gloomy light in the stairwell, I liked the heavy door to the building, I liked everything strange and odd and even brutal about the place, because it was unlike New Zealand. And that's what I was looking for. Even so, homesickness, the desire for a beach, a flaxy hillside, my friends and family, had to be negotiated, that sudden ache. Emma and Pete asked me if I would stay on to nanny their two-year-old son, Leon – a lively and beautiful fair-haired boy who spoke German-infused English – so that Emma could go back to work part time, and I agreed. The couple were old enough to seem proper adults to me, and also young enough to party with. We sat up late talking about Hitler and Germany and New Zealand and religion; we listened to Pink Floyd and the Rolling Stones, watched Monty Python movies, or, when Pete had gone to bed, Emma and I watched sad movies like the one about the priest who saves orphans in Mexico. Their German friend, Hans, turned up early one morning while I was still in bed on the couch. I heard the knock, and I heard Pete getting out of bed to let him in. They came quietly into the living room to get to the kitchen to make coffee, and I heard Hans pause beside my bed and indicate to Pete that he thought I looked good. Pete agreed, sounding embarrassed. Hans was my father's age.

One day Emma, Leon and I were in the city centre, wandering around a picturesque square where there was a man playing piano accordion, and a little girl playing a tiny cello, and a beautiful young man dressed in white playing a recorder. There were fruit stalls piled high with cherries and strawberries. I was very tired all of a sudden; I felt as though I was hallucinating it all. I also felt exhausted by the straightforwardness of Germans, how they carry their bodies in their words, and always get just a little bit too close when they share their opinions or ask something. It is so strange to me, the formality and the fleshiness. It's there in Katherine Mansfield's story from *In a German Pension*, 'Germans at Meat':

> Bread soup was placed upon the table.
> 'Ah,' said the Herr Rat, leaning upon the table as he peered into the tureen, 'that is what I need. My "magen" has not been in order for several days. Bread soup, and just the right consistency. I am a good cook myself' – he turned to me.
> 'How interesting,' I said, attempting to infuse just the right amount of enthusiasm into my voice.

Emma and Pete asked if I'd like to come with them on a three-week holiday to Turkey. They would be taking their campervan and Hans would take his; he would be travelling with two of his daughters. I desperately wanted to see Turkey.

Before going away, we visited Hans and his wife, Jan, in their old, whitewashed farmhouse which sat amongst rolling hills and forest about three hours out of Munich. One room in their house was floor-to-ceiling books in German and English, classical music cassettes and records. One of Hans's records was a recording of speeches by Hitler. On its cover Hitler is sitting on a chair with a blonde-haired little girl on his lap. Hans was an antique dealer, so the house was full of fascinating things. He had two parrots who sat on his shoulders and ate food from his mouth. We had stuffed red peppers and a brown rice salad for dinner, at a long wooden table with tall candles flickering at its centre. We stayed the night, and my room was a low-roofed bedroom at the top of a set of narrow stairs. Hans's wife Jan was an English woman, younger than him, who seemed both sad and angry most of the time. Her face had a hectic look to it. Perhaps my face looked like that many years later, when I too was in an impossible relationship that had some unarguably beautiful architecture around it.

We left for our trip to Turkey, the two large and beautifully equipped campervans in convoy: me, Leon, Pete and Emma in one and Hans and two of his daughters in the other. When we reached Yugoslavia, we took a highway, known in the communist era as the Brotherhood and Unity Highway, down the centre of the country. At night we camped, sometimes not far from Roma camps, and Hans and I were often the last two awake, outside in this bare-feeling land talking and talking.

The further into Yugoslavia we drove, the further back in time we seemed to move. There were women in long dresses and scarves, and horse and carts, old shepherds with small flocks of sheep, and everywhere children asking for cigarettes. On the roadsides there were lonely and fragrant fruit stands. On the endless stretches of road were billboards with Tito's serious and beloved face on them. We travelled on that long central transit road through Yugoslavia, me sleeping in a tent with Hans's daughter, Lina, who occasionally gave me a funny look, not in dislike but as though we shared a secret. She would smile a small smile. She was from Hans's second marriage, and

I don't think she liked Jan, the third wife, so maybe in her mind we were accomplices in undermining her. Sometimes Lina and I swam together in rivers. In the tent that we shared she slept with a gun close to her pillow to scare off wild dogs. If my life in New Zealand hadn't prepared me for this country and this experience, my reading life had. For me the danger wasn't in sleeping in a tent in Yugoslavia next to a girl with a gun whose father was coming on to me, the danger was in turning away from risk and going back to something ordinary.

We travelled through Skopje and camped at the Vardar River by the Greek border where I wrote in my diary that *there is a bit of tension amongst us all at the moment*, and I think by this point, Hans and I had started our affair.

I was wilfully outside of time. I was involved with a charming man whose home held hundreds of books and walls full of classical music (forget about that one album with the blonde girl on it). I thought we got each other (we absolutely didn't). He told me he liked me with my long curly hair tied back. He supported me when Emma was angry with me for something. Hans was used to being in the world, dealing in its treasures. I was 19 and, although not blameless, certainly naïve. And hungry. Sitting outside until the stars brightened, cloaking the bare hills, and then fading into pink and orange skies. Hans took offence easily. He liked me in my floaty hippy dresses, but I was more comfortable in cut-off jeans. I would almost have given my right arm to keep the freedom I was enjoying. I was one of his treasures. I was loving being out in the world.

I wrote in my diary that *I never want to leave Turkey*. I loved its colours, its spice-rich air, its open-all-hours chai houses, its food, its beaches, its warm bustling evenings, its deep nights, its sunflowers. Because Hans and Pete and Emma had travelled there often and knew it well, we got to travel off the beaten track. A huge orange sun set nightly into the Marmara Sea, the Black Sea, the Aegean. We crossed the Bosphorus from Anatolia to Thrace. From Europe to Asia. Late one night Hans drove us to see the shining mosques of Istanbul. I wrote in my diary that mosques, especially at night, must have the most beautiful architecture in the world.

Seven years later, when I was a mother, married to Kester, we took a trip with Elliot to Europe and visited Emma and Pete in Munich. They talked about Hans, and how he killed himself. It happened just before we left New Zealand, but my parents didn't tell me for fear of me being upset when we were just heading off (my mother guessed there had been something between Hans and me). Anyway, they didn't say, and so I heard it there, in the apartment where I first met him. It was winter in Munich, and everything was frozen, including the fountains: the water frozen in its flow between slim upraised arms, small bare breasts, fish, mermaids, gargoyles, and the bowl for catching and releasing. I thought of the record with Hitler and the little girl on its cover. We left Emma and Pete's and went to the München Hauptbanhof to travel somewhere else, and I got a terrible migraine. A kind German doctor looked after me.

Craigievar castle – a legend

I talk about my Great-Uncle Jim taking me to visit Craigievar castle at the start of the previous section, and my 19-year-old-self gives a very skimpy description of it in her diary. So, to expand on the tartan upholstery and the haunted feeling, here is a small legend.

> Craigievar is a seven-storey, pink, turreted castle, one of the prettiest in Aberdeenshire, reputed to be a model for Walt Disney's *Cinderella* castle. The legend of Craigievar explains the motto that appears here and there inside the castle: *Doe not vaken sleiping dogs*. Sir John Forbes became the laird of Craigievar Castle in 1648, but when he was a child in the castle, he adored the family's two hounds Ferelith and Fintray, and liked to snuggle in with them as they slept by the fire. He was upset when, every night, his father sent them out to the kennels, saying 'The horse to its stable. The hawk to its perch. The dog to its kennel.' On a very cold snowy night, wearing just a night shirt, and in bare feet, young John snuck outside to let them back into the castle, but lost his way, fell down and was soon covered with snow. It was the hounds, Ferelith and Fintray, who alerted young John's parents, who were so relieved not to have lost their son that they henceforth always let the hounds sleep inside by the fire, their son curled up beside them. When young John became laird of the castle, he took for his motto *Doe not vaken sleiping dogs* because dogs also deserve to sleep where it is warm. The castle is said to be haunted by a fiddler who drowned in a well in the kitchen, and a Gordon who was thrust through the window of the Blue Room.

Three

A house in the landscape

I am 23 and soon I will be married

There is a photo of me taken in 1982 at the top of the Remutaka Hill summit, 555 meters above sea level, the Hutt Valley and Wellington to one side, and the Wairarapa to the other. It is a typically wild and windy day. Kester and I have parked at the lookout, crossed the road and started a walk along one of the paths into the hills. In the photo I have turned to look back and he has snapped me. My hair is tearing off to the side, my loose pink jumper is slammed against one side of my body, I am caught in mid movement, sculpted by wind, and I am looking fierce. Kester is handsome and strong and not feeling the cold in a T-shirt and shorts, and he has supplies in his backpack (a thermos of tea, gingernuts, apples). 'Gotcha' he says, smiling. We are walking into typically dense New Zealand bush, which is bent towards the ground by the constant wind. We disturb the tiny dusty branches and star flowers of the mānuka, we push back the supplejack and brush past the ferns. Trees start to throw shade across us. The disappearing sky flaps like a flag far above our heads, and we are watching where we put our feet. We make our way in and through.

There is often, for me, a profound sense of isolation in the New Zealand bush. Jane Campion and Vincent Ward were not wrong. There are plenty of places where you can walk into the bush and keep walking and not meet another person for three or four days. Kester liked this. Days into a tramp he could throw his pack into a river and swim after it to get somewhere that was circled on a swirling map inside a plastic bag inside the pack. I am not like that. It cramps my chest to think of such risk in such isolation. That is not my kind of outdoors.

At the time of this photograph, where I frown towards the camera through wind and space and the dust of shaking groundcover, I was also trying to build a writing life in

Wellington, including organising a series of poetry readings at Circa Theatre. I was the barefoot MC facilitating the open mic and introducing feature poets: Bill Manhire, Cilla McQueen, Harry Ricketts, Fleur Adcock, Lauris Edmond, Louis Johnson, David Eggleton, Ian Wedde, Murray Edmond and Sam Hunt. In the interval between the open mic and the feature poet, my sister Clare would play guitar and sing. We were raised to perform, starting with our family accordion band (joining not optional), and so it wasn't strange for us to 'put on shows'. We'd been doing it our whole lives, as long as we'd been strong enough to stand up straight with an accordion hanging from our shoulders (which is possible from age five). And as if this degree of childhood performance wasn't enough, with the neighbouring kids we put on plays for our parents: *The Little Mermaid* (A woman must suffer in order to be beautiful) and the musical *Oliver!* (Where is love?). In the early 80s I put all of this performing experience into something that I wanted to make happen: a platform for live poetry readings in Wellington.

I had spent the previous year living on Grafton Road in Auckland. While I was there, I was a regular reader and one-time guest poet at David Mitchell's *Poetry Live!* sessions at the Globe, a pub on Wakefield Street. It was an intense and enlivening time to be living in Auckland, not least because of those diverse and exciting poetry readings. It was the time of the anti-apartheid Springbok Tour protests, and I felt the power of communal action. Coming back to Wellington, fired up from my time in Auckland, I started the monthly Circa Theatre poetry readings.* But at the same time as I stepped

---

* Quite recently, and out of the blue, poet and writer David Howard emailed me about those poetry readings at Circa Theatre: '[Y]our brave venture was pivotal for me. It would be years (1985) before I felt confident or desperate enough to give my first public reading. But having heard these people was essential to my understanding of what was possible in contemporary poetry.'

deeper into my writing life, another pressure rose up in me. I remember sitting at the long, busy table in my parents' house, a fire flickering in the background, some infants wriggling on some knees, good food in good pottery at the centre of the table, hands dishing up, hands pouring wine, and my father saying to me, half-jokingly, that I am past the first flush of youth, and then something about not leaving it too long to get married. In the photograph at the top of the Remutaka Hill, I look both fierce and anxious: this is a photo of me in the process of upsetting my own applecart by deciding to marry when I was not ready, knowing what I was doing, feeling guilty about it, but mostly feeling shattered by this deep subversion of self. Kester, my husband to be, a chemical engineer, had applied for a job at Petralgas in Taranaki. I did not feel seen, but I did feel captured.

Equal shares

I lift half a teaspoon of fluffy white baked potato to my mouth and swallow it. I was almost four months pregnant with my second child. The day-long throwing up hadn't stopped, and I was thin, still at my pre-pregnancy weight. My doctor was starting to talk about a hospital stay. So, the teaspoon and the potato.

Because I couldn't face it, my partner Bennett had to cook for Elliot, who was five. I heard him speak to Elliot in a patronising tone. I heard the two of them getting upset in their very different ways: Elliot spilling over and Bennett drawing in, becoming more clipped. I balanced a few peas on my spoon and lifted them to my mouth. Peas – three, two, one. Tears – one, two, three, four. After he'd eaten his dinner, Elliot came to lie beside me on the bed. Bennett believed he was doing a good job – setting limits and slowly explaining the why of his decisions to Elliot. But his tone was infuriating, so Elliot was infuriated by it, as was I. After Elliot went to bed, we fought, and Bennett then used 'the tone' on me: *I know you are* very *protective of your son.* Our fighting woke Elliot, who stood in the doorway of the living room and asked us if it was morning yet.

I had a rough birth with Tamara. One morning a few days after the birth, I woke up, looked over to the bassinette, and couldn't remember if I'd had a girl or a boy. I lay there with my heart thumping. Days later, when someone stopped me in the street to admire Tamara and ask what her name was, I couldn't think of it. Embarrassing moments passed and I was almost ready to make one up when her name, the beautiful Hebrew name that means date palm in a desert, came back to me. *Her name is Tamara.*

Some months after Tamara's birth, in an effort to recreate the outside world, I said that I would like a newspaper subscription, but Bennett vetoed it, saying that, until I was earning, I didn't have the financial autonomy to make that decision. Around the same time he suggested that, until we had equal shares of money in the house, we wouldn't be equal in our relationship. Which meant we would never be equal. I thought about how I had come into the relationship already a single mother, and I wondered what he had imagined about us, our lives together, our growing family.

The stress of Bennett's controlling behaviour, my slow recovery from the birth, and my anxiety for Elliot, who was not doing well, made eczema flare on the palms of my hands. I scratched and scratched, and they cracked and bled. At night, when the itching was unbearable, I stood in the bathroom with my hands in a basin of cold water. Someone suggested a homeopathic remedy, and I just looked at them for a while. I wanted to tell them that the cracks in my palms were my rage breaking out, so they should be careful about sharing their ridiculous suggestions. But actually, I *had* tried homeopathic remedies, even though I knew they wouldn't work. I had tried everything. Nothing worked until, when Tamara was 18 months old, I left Bennett. Within days of shifting out, my eczema had gone. I could dress myself and Tamara with ease. I could do the dishes without pain. I could peel an orange. I could handle things again.

We regrouped as a family, the three of us, and although we were stepping into a life of perilous finances, a small, intimate, precious peace held us, and we breathed out. Then one day, Bennett didn't return Tamara at the agreed time. He had decided he would keep them three nights of the week he told me, including every weekend, and a new sort of purgatory began.

It was hard for me to cope with this sudden and unnegotiated extended separation from my child, and as I practised moving through the world without them for almost half of each week, I was in an alternate universe where nothing was as it should be.

*

I don't know what else to say about this time in my life, except that I gave myself away – as per the instructions of my life-training. Like so many women of my generation, I did not get a mandate for the authoritative gesture, the line in the sand. I would like my stronger self with her lately acquired survival skills to tell my younger, suffering self that there is a better future ahead, and I am holding her a seat at the table.

This is also true

A few years ago, when Tamara was caring for Bennett at his home and then in the hospital when he was dying, a significant part of their work was balancing Bennett's need for rest with the visits from his many friends who wanted to spend time with him.

From the darkness outside

It is 1995, I am a single parent of two, and I'm walking the kids to school. Elliot tears ahead of me on his bike, disappearing around a sharp corner, and I call after him to slow down, which he ignores. I hold Tamara's hand. They are walking incredibly slowly because their 13 imaginary friends are, as ever, coming with us, and the two youngest are babies and can only crawl. I suggest they might want to go in an imaginary pushchair, but Tamara says they want to crawl. I used to walk to primary school on this same street, beside the low fence with its wooden framing and wire mesh intertwined with bridal veil roses. We would break thorns off the stems and balance them on our noses like rhino-children. And suddenly I am there, walking to school in the rain in my long red and green tartan raincoat, picking a thorn off a dark red stem with slippery fingers and sticking it on my wet nose. The prickliness of the task, the cold, the rain, the potential for wet fingers to slip onto the sharp tip of the thorn, are all part of the joy. The world so present, so textured, so interactive. And down the beach road, not far from us, the sea thudding and crashing and stinking of seaweed and why were we going to school instead of being let loose to play? Tamara would also rather play outside, their smallest imaginary children slowing down the moment of settling into their Year One classroom, and Elliot, who is nearly finished with primary school, on his bike, trying to outrun it.

For my kids, growing up in the small town of Pukerua Bay, there was community and there was outside. In the midst of difficulty, it was plenty. It was more than plenty, it was marvellous. But it had taken us a while to find our feet.

After I left Bennett, we shifted into Wellington city, to a house that had been cut into four flats in an ugly fashion so that no room felt whole or undissected. A solitary man in army fatigues who ordered gun catalogues lived downstairs and he didn't like the noise of children. He banged on his ceiling with something – a broom or a gun – when they were noisy. One night when Tamara was crying, the woman in the adjoining flat pressed her face to the front door. The glass in the door was textured and because of that her face looked partly melted, and it terrified me. When the kids weren't home, I went running – the only time in my life when I have been a runner – and as I ran past lovely Wellington villas, I would imagine living in just such a house with the harbour shimmering in the background. Why couldn't I take part in the world instead of shaking coins out of my wallet to buy milk. Poverty is pervasive. There's no place in your life that it doesn't get into, and it hurts everyone it touches. I took that ugly flat in a daze, just because it was available, and because I couldn't imagine that I deserved anything better, which is the gift you come away with when you've been in an abusive relationship. I left Bennett before the 2001 Property (Relationships) Amendment Act came into effect, and neither Kester nor Bennett paid child support, so renting, and its attendant wild card situations, was the reality for us. But, despite the depressing flat and my exhaustion and my guilt for not being able to hold a family together for my children, a part of me felt elated. I could find my own shape again, listen to my own thoughts. Begin to trust myself. Despite that sawn-off unloved and unlovely flat, the kids and I began to relax, sensing that there was space there for all of us.

It was in my little Edinburgh flat, in the unnervingly spacious quiet of lockdown, that I first read Rachel Cusk's *Coventry*, where, in her essay 'Aftermath', she writes about leaving her husband and shifting into a new flat, and how, one winter's night she walked with her children to a carol service. At the service, she looks around at the other families and thinks 'it is like looking at them through a brightly lit window from the darkness outside' and that those spot-lit families play their roles with the 'whole world as a backdrop'. She writes that she and her children are no longer part of that story. She and her children are now part of the risky, fragmented, disordered outside world, with its accompanying whiff of freedom. She writes that if the world is constantly evolving, the family is not, the family tries to stay the same: 'A house in the landscape,' she writes, 'both shelter and prison.'

I agree with Cusk that the family endeavours to stay the same. The family is by design conservative. And a resounding *yes* to the newly single parent no longer being part of the lit-up and orderly world. *Yes* to that feeling of being outside, looking in, no longer belonging to the service, the singing, or the song. And *yes* to how, particularly if you are a woman, living in the risky, more disorderly world can feel like the gaining of freedom. *Yes*, to the unchanging house in the landscape being potentially both shelter and prison. And when you leave it, you step into the dark, with the dark's particular freedoms and perils.

Jacqueline Rose's book *Mothers: An Essay on Love and Cruelty* unpacks an inherent belief that, as she puts it, mothers are tasked to fix everything that is wrong in the world because they are the cause of it. The impossible tail-eating burden of this argument is explored in an essay under the section entitled 'Social Punishment', where Rose writes about the vilification of single mothers. She suggests that there is a link between society's expectation on mothers generally to be wholly devoted to the task of mothering, and the fact that a single mother, by necessity, obeys this directive 'to the letter'. Rose writes that the single mother brings 'too close to the surface the utter craziness, not to say the unmanageable nature, of the idea that a mother should exist for her child and nothing else'.

I think of how, as a single parent, when I needed to defend

myself in the Family Court, I could hardly speak. How the clothes I had carefully chosen suddenly felt wrong, as if my black skirt and green cardigan were chosen to allure and not to present me as part of the serious adult world. Why at that moment did my clothes seem to shapeshift? Was it that I was outside of the framework of the two-parent family, and so somewhere in my own conflicted head, beyond the pale. And could it be that I felt that *despite everything* I was a good mother. Was it a good mother the judge looked at when it was my turn to speak? I was trying not to feel like a single mother. I was trying to feel like *something better than that.* Not somebody whose life had become 24-hour-a-day mothering. Something as well as that. A good mother *and* a citizen of the world. Somebody you could take seriously.

The impossible tale-eating burden of this story.

Whose benefit?

I was walking along a street in Wellington a few years back, and a woman walked towards me with two children, around four and eight, at either side of her. On her face was an expression that I knew because I've worn that expression. That is the face of someone who has bills at home that she can't pay, whose flat is hard to heat, and who doesn't have the money for the school trip that's coming up; whose clothes are the kind of no-colour of old, cheap clothes, and who keeps a blank face when some well-meaning friend says, *Just tell me if you need anything*, because despite visiting the food bank for the first time in her life last week, and that food eaten, and the power still not paid, and she needs shoes for the kids, and the boy's birthday coming up, despite all that, there's nothing to ask for. You can't ask for a decent living wage for this 24-hour-a-day unpaid work. You can't ask for a tank of petrol or a ten-trip train ticket. You can't even ask someone to buy you a family size block of cheese (what a gift that would be!). You can't. It's just better if they don't offer. One time she is so pushed that she phones someone who offered that if you need to go shopping just call and they'll give you a lift, but it turns out they can't that day and she puts down the phone with her face burning. There is no entry to the maze she is in. No one can meet you there who isn't there themself.

On the street in Wellington her kids float along behind her, making a little girl-and-boy-sized wake, with little boy-and-girl expressions of anxiety. It's a treat to be in town, or should be, but nothing flows. Mum sits in McDonald's pretending not to be hungry so that they can have a McDonald's lunch. Mum sips her coffee. Their treat has a particular glitch, a halt, a misstep. If it's a treat shouldn't Mum's face also be relaxed and pleased, not this ceramic mask. Shouldn't she eat? She walks fast, fast down the street, the little girl grabs at her hand and says, *Wait*.

She can't keep up. But the mother can't stop because. She can't stop. She's furious. It breaks her heart when her daughter says to slow down, and when the girl starts to cry that thin cry, she just wishes they were all back home having Milo. What is the point in going out? She aches for adult company, to be with friends, to enjoy buying and wrapping presents for her boy, to anticipate with pleasure those things that are meant to be a pleasure. A gift. A way to love somebody.

If he would just pay child support, she could transition into paid work. But he won't, even though he easily could with his professional job and his holidays abroad. He has the children three nights a week which means he doesn't have to pay child support. He genuinely wants to have them. He also genuinely doesn't want to pay child support. Or offer any other financial support. Or compromise his full-time work which is why he insisted on having the children across weekends. Now that they've been through mediation and the Family Court, they share weekends. It took a lot of effort. It took a big toll. In this land of milk and honey her sky is falling in like wet cardboard.

They had financially comfortable lives until she was a single parent. Now, day after week after month after year, she and the children barely survive.

Vida & me

One mild summer day I was walking through the Meadows in Edinburgh – that piece of historically common land – and there were students and families picnicking in the elm and cherry tree-lined meadows, when out of the blue I bumped into my 19-year-old self. Our shoulders glancing off each other, her quick impatient look, my quick-stop heart. Oh, love. *Living*, she whispered as she passed, *where I should have lived*. If, at 19, I had stayed in Europe. If I hadn't gone back. And she scoots off to sit with friends, leaving me with this overwhelming feeling that she is right, that this is where I should have lived. I looked at her, leaning away from me and towards them, her fellow students in their circle on the grass, fur around the jacket hood, jeans, a slumped bag fat with books, wine in a plastic cup. They talked about. It's not my business to know what they talked about, but worlds were being unpacked. *Hello, self that didn't self-destruct*. And yes, of course, I know she'd still have to hurt and fall, we all have to grow up. But what could she have been if I'd had the wherewithal to make my life there, then. *At 19*, Vida said, her hand softly on my arm, *I was getting married to Henry to escape my parents! What did we know? All we had was a longing that we couldn't name*. And Vida pulled me back, and there were no families picnicking under the trees, no students gathering in circles, just individual households: parents and their particular kids, couples, single people, all trying not to get too close, all trying not to touch each other. Not talking across spaces. Masks like paper hands across their faces. Then, for the first time in what felt like ages, a piper in a kilt stood at the centre of the Meadows and started to play: *Flower of Scotland, Scotland the Brave, Amazing Grace*.

Four

Disturbing the air

Nameless little rivers

> Star of Bethlehem flowers clustered together in groups, like milestones flashing along the way. Hawthorn wound itself in thorny whiteness, smelling like heartbreak, if heartbreak could smell.
> —Jessie Kesson, *The White Bird Passes*

To get to Muirhouse Library, you walked through a derelict, semi-enclosed, mostly shut down shopping centre. The gents at the back of the bookies were the setting for the memorable overflowing toilet scene in *Trainspotting*. Concrete bollards in bright colours memorialised the individual shops that once serviced the community with fruit and vegetables, groceries and meat, with quotes from locals about what the shops had meant to them. One remembered the fruit and veg shop where 'the lady who worked there let my toddler son play with the potatoes'. A few months after I started working for Muirhouse Library, all of the empty shops were torn down, along with the bollards, to make space for a small Tesco, and a courtyard. While the Tesco still didn't bring much in the way of fresh food to the area, it was an improvement on the ghost shopping centre with its shuttered black roller doors.

In the months when things were being torn down and then built, there was a makeshift plywood tunnel from the road to the library. The tunnel was painted such a dark blue that it turned to black a few feet in. A newsagent and an African goods shop were the only stores still open, and these were within the tunnel. Sometimes a growling pit bull sat outside the newsagent waiting for its owner, and you had to edge past it, eyes lowered and fingers crossed. Sometimes pigeons flew through the tunnel, swishing past your face with a dusty flurry of wings. Sometimes a ghost in a grey tracksuit walked towards you. Or an angry girl with a pram. Or a group of wild-energy tracksuited boys on bikes – swerving, standing on the pedals, shouting. Their faces sharp, hungry, shuttered, manic, furious. When you reached the end of the tunnel, you walked through billowing crisp wrappers, plastic bottles, energy drink cans and cigarette butts to get to the library, where you might find that the external roller door had been kicked in, or the bins set on fire.

There were always kids in the library. Primary and secondary school kids came in to use the computers, to gather in groups with friends, to colour in, and to give cheek to staff, but plenty of them arrived every day to create some kind of chaos, like riding their bikes into the library, or throwing chairs, or starting fights. As far as I could see, library staff looked after the kids as well as anyone did. And the kids were in the library whenever school was out. I lasted six months at Muirhouse, until my colleague was attacked by a teenage boy. She left the job, and I asked to be transferred. It isn't the awful fact of my colleague, a young mother, being attacked that really stays with me. What haunts me is seeing a big man leaning over his toddler son who was lying on his back on the floor – the man's clenched fist an inch or so above the child's face – telling him over and over in a flat and furious voice to *get up*. But it's not even that; it's what rises above that. Despite living in a place where violence was the dominant language, so many of the kids and their parents still found the energy to be generous and funny and brave. Nobody signs up for or wants that sort of life. It's luck. And above that, it is systems.

*

The wood thickened and dimmed. Great patches of wild hyacinths waved darkly blue. The sky was crowded out. Moss sprang beneath their feet, and the dust of

it rose like thin smoke. The foosty guff of an ancient wood drifted over and past in great imprisoning waves.
—Jessie Kesson, *The White Bird Passes*

*

I had my own small experience of coming up against systems that don't or won't see you. During the custody dispute with Bennett, I had to take my kids to a social worker at a Child and Family Centre in Porirua, about 19 kilometres from where I lived. I was on the Domestic Purposes Benefit (as it was known then), and every journey in the car was considered, because petrol was always short. That morning I had turned up at the Centre with Elliot and Tamara and we were waiting to be seen. Our social worker walked by with a co-worker. The co-worker asked her if she wanted coffee, our social worker glanced at her watch and said she would because her next family (us) were always late. We weren't, I made sure of that. We were sitting there, the three of us, knee-deep in anxiety and vulnerability, and this woman was lying about us. It was a glib and easy lie, one you might make to a friend to smooth the way towards a fun activity: 'No, I've got nothing else on,' 'They won't mind,' 'Yes, I've got time for that coffee.' Or maybe it's what the social worker expected, even if it wasn't what happened. Sitting there and not being seen was shameful, and then, very quickly, infuriating. I stood up and spoke to the social worker's back, telling her we were there, and *we* had been waiting for *her*. I was flooded with fury. It took years for that fury to properly drain away. I tried to imagine what would be required for the people I was meeting in Muirhouse to move beyond fury, without falling into that other bear-pit, shame and despair. For furies, layered furies, to properly drain away, you need to gain control of your life, even in just one or two areas. You have to pull away from damaging families and from the community that loved and hurt you. You have to step into a world you haven't been prepared for, with nothing in your pocket. It requires a virtuoso performance of self.

*

> The great fir wood of Laveroch shadowed the road; yellow primroses and blue vetch lost their own colour in its shadow, pale, like the wood's own wild, white anemones drifting down the banks.
> —Jessie Kesson, *The White Bird Passes*

*

After I asked to be transferred from Muirhouse, Edinburgh Libraries sent me to Granton Library, less than a mile down the road. It was a smaller library and wasn't so comprehensively held to ransom by lost youth and children, although it was dangerous enough at times. I grew to love Granton Library, both the staff and the people who used the library and brought with them knitting, snacks to share, photos of children, children themselves, visiting relatives, and entertaining stories.

Over the two years that I was at Granton Library I worked with Lorrane, an adult literacy educator from the Royston Wardieburn Community Centre, not far from us. I ran creative writing workshops for her small adult literacy group. The women in the group ranged in age from 40s to 70s and were all local. Three of the four members are now diagnosed with dyslexia but had battled through the school system without a diagnosis: sitting at the back of the class, thought to be stupid, believing they were stupid. Unable to write because the words wouldn't keep still, because the words sometimes visibly hung in the air but didn't make it onto the page. For them, pens and pages and books and words were anxiety-provoking and shaming.

What started as a single six-week course ran for two years. Greta, a great-grandmother, was dropped off and picked up each week by her family. When it came time to read out her work, Greta apologised for everything she had written, and in the next breath she marvelled at being able to write at all, let alone tell her own story. Just weeks into the course she began to write a sentence or two about her garden or her family, and one day she wrote a piece several sentences long that moved between her street and its people and her garden. She had, for the first time, taken us on a journey. If I am making the work sound childish, I don't mean to. Greta was deeply embedded in community, in place, and in family, and this came through in her work: there was her rootedness, her sense of being part of things.

Sharing and listening to stories became the central pillar for the group. When they wrote evaluations, they'd mention the joy of listening to each other's stories, of writing about their world, and of being part of a supportive group. They'd talk about the power of putting words onto the page. Greta told us her family noticed a change in her, that she was more confident. Another member, Marnie, said that she noticed so much more now when she was out walking, and that as she walked, she would think how she would write about what she was seeing. Over the two years of classes, Lorrane and I watched in awe as Marnie stepped into a writing life that seemed to have been waiting for her. I imagine she still walks and looks, and that in the rhythm of walking and looking, stories come to her, day by day, movement by movement.

Starting out, my idea for the class was simple. I would try to dismantle every hurdle that I could imagine was standing between these people and the page, so spelling and grammar and sentence structure were out the window. There was no comparing, no word count, no negative feedback; in fact there were just shared talks, short writing exercises, and the reading out of work. Lorrane ensured that they had the appropriate coloured paper, so the words wouldn't dance around on the page, and that I delivered the class at a certain pace. She was great at checking in without interrupting the flow or fracturing a good atmosphere. We both looked for excerpts of stories and poems for the class. Lorrane found beautiful poems in Scots by writers like Tom Leonard and Edwin Morgan. I gave short talks on technique illustrated by a reading from books that I thought they'd enjoy. For example, I talked about imagery and finding treasure in unlikely places, and I read the opening paragraphs from Janet Frame's *Owls Do Cry* where the four siblings, Chicks, Daphne, Toby, and Francie, are finding treasure at the dump – for them a magical place edged with 'a gold tickle of toi-toi'. They sit in a 'hollow of refuse', and in this 'living and lived-in wound' the children first find fairy tales.

The group's response to any reading was wholehearted, but for it to work for them it had to work emotionally as well as critically (Frame passed with flying colours). They were not afraid to tell us if they didn't like a certain poem or story, and why. But more than anything, they supported us: by being kind when we tripped up, by 'holding' the group in their very practised hands, and telling us, constantly and with great surprise, how much they were enjoying writing. It took some courage for them to put pen to paper, and we couldn't have brought creative writing to them if they hadn't, despite a painful history of perceived failure, met us halfway.

I kept working with the group after I left Granton Library. We were funded for some more sessions, and I enjoyed the teaching and the chance to keep in contact with friends at the library. But then, Covid happened. I thought this was the end, for the time being, of the creative writing classes. But I underestimated the group, and Lorrane's commitment to keeping the classes going. So, despite a general unease with things technical, the group agreed to attend classes online. This required a lot of assistance from Lorrane, who got them connected and on screen so they could arrive in the living room of my flat once a week, and where my lonesome heart would be lifted by their virtual presence. For the online classes, I recorded and posted a five-minute video, which would include a reading, a talk about something that sprang from the reading, and a writing exercise, then a few days later we would meet online to talk about the reading and share their writing.

One reading I did was from the autobiographical novel *The White Bird Passes* by Scottish writer Jessie Kesson. The book, set in the 1920s, tells the story of Janie, who was born into 'The Lane' in a very poor part of an unnamed city in Scotland. Janie's beautiful and fiery mother, Liza, made her money as a sex worker, and on good days she would tell Janie wonderful stories, especially on their occasional long walk out of the city and through the countryside to visit Liza's mother, who was austere but loving, and her father, who wouldn't speak to Liza or to Janie. But one day the worst happened, and the 'cruelty man' came to The Lane. He looked at their life and judged Janie's mother unfit, and Janie was taken away to an orphanage in the shadow of the Cairngorm mountains in Aberdeenshire. The language of the novel is luminous, and the story gritty. The women from Granton leaned towards this novel the way a willow leans towards water. I read to them about Janie and her mother walking, one late summer's day, to Janie's grandparents' home, and how they notice the flowers on their way. The flowers have resonant names like Snow in Summer and Dead Man's Bells and Love in a Mist. Janie loves it when her mother casts a practised eye over the brambles and says, 'We'll need to come for a day in autumn for the bramble picking', because although

Janie knows they won't, she 'had learned to enjoy the prospect more than the reality.'

The group nodded in recognition at the flowers, and talked about their own walks to find wild flowers, where you might find them now and where you used to find them, and how wild flowers were more of a surprise, somehow, than the garden-grown variety. *The White Bird Passes* is a powerful Scottish story studded with fragments of the songs and poems that Liza taught to Janie, and that Liza would have learned from her parents, and so on. On the hard day when a ravaged Liza tries to convince the orphanage to let the now teenage Janie come home to look after her by showing a doctor's note that says she has advanced syphilis (not realising what this meant), Janie's heart breaks. She remembers how her beautiful mother once:

> gave the nameless little rivers high hill sources and deep sea endings. She put a singing seal in Loch Na Boune and a lament on the long, lonely winds. She saw a legend in the canna flowers and a plough amongst the stars.

Janie didn't go back to The Lane. If Liza's father would have been kind and taken them in, or if the 'cruelty man' would have kept away, if Scots hadn't been for the simmering fights and English for a bloodless politeness, if Janie had been left to go on living in The Lane, hungry, underdressed, joyfully imaginative, surviving on a kind of slap-dash communal care, how might it have ended? Would Janie/Jessie have become a writer? I guess, for better or for worse outcomes, it would have been less painful. *The White Bird Passes* led to some vivid, lively, sad, and funny recollections in our group – it spoke to them in both its attention to beauty and to community, and in its deep, honest look into poverty.

Marnie never liked to write about personal things, or sad

things. We respected this, and her writing was, anyway, such an original picture of the world she walked through that no one wanted to get in the way of it. And then one day she wrote this poem about a time in her childhood when her family were moved from a council flat in Greendykes into a tower block:

Just Livin

The flats, the multies, the high-rise
It's the 80's
You can say what you like
Punks with mohicans
They're not gonna bite

Glue sniffers buzzin
Lifts stinkin eh piss
Stairs are no better
You're takin a risk

The view is spectacular
From this great height
Bairns pushin bairns
Some play on their bikes

Some chasin demons
A dragon or two
Some chase their wives
Screamin into the loo

The phone box is ringin
They shout up to tell
Take a message ya numpty
Am up here in hell

When Marnie brought this poem to the class and read it out, we all sat stunned and momentarily silenced. Here was a poem from the hinterland of experience, from the 'foosty guff' that lifted underfoot as she walked through her own remembered forest. It is a poem written in the long, long tradition of the Scottish ballad – the communal song – but it sings a story of displacement from the flow of community. It sings a story of nameless little rivers with no high hill sources or deep sea endings.

Summer, 2019

George, who lived in the flat opposite mine, sharing the narrow, gabled top of our tenement, is dead. He jumped out of his window, out onto the Royal Mile. The police told me this when they turned up at my door one evening and invited themselves inside. About two hours after the police left, someone pressed the outside buzzer for my flat. I walked to my intercom and looked at it. I thought about George, so wired and thin, his shaved and tattooed head and neck, the way one day he bolted past me on the stairs, the look on his face as though the devil were chasing him. How he sometimes had rough sleepers to stay and how, sometimes, when those rough sleepers rang my buzzer by mistake, I answered, and they said *Hi Pal, can you buzz me in* and then other more desperate stuff. I didn't let them in. George's wired energy frightened me. And yet, one day when a fold-up cube bed arrived for me when I wasn't home, he looked after it for me, and I thought maybe he took it for his homeless friends to sleep on. But he was holding it for me. And when he passed it over, he kind of apologised for his kindness, as though I was bound to be thinking what I had been thinking.

I would say *Hi* and he'd say *Hi Pal* when we passed each other on the stairs. But he frightened me. Although not enough for me to leave. Because I loved my flat. A bunch of yellow flowers appeared against the side of the building below his high window. I think his son and daughter-in-law left the flowers there.

*

A few days later, there was a stabbing in a park near Granton Library. More police. And cordoned-off blocks of flats.

*

The same summer, a woman attacked another woman in the library, a mother attacked a mother, because a Scottish woman from the grey flats across the road thought the Czech woman had told her kid off. When the Scottish woman confronted her, the Czech woman said yes, she had, but only gently. The woman's boy was hurting her boy. The Czech woman wasn't scared, but I would have been. The Scottish woman flew towards the Czech woman and started punching her in the face. Other library workers rushed in to break up the fight. But not me. I thought, I don't get paid enough for this.

*

During that summer I finally took the time to learn the shape for the wax and wane of the moon. A waxing moon has darkness on the left. A waning moon has darkness on the right.

In the absence of the otter

I caught a bus from the centre of Edinburgh out to Musselburgh because I wanted to walk by the River Esk and wash some clouds out of my head. I wanted birds over brute words (there'd been some violence at work). I wanted birds over buses, their stops and starts, and the deep anxious sound of suitcases being wheeled places, which is the ground note, the *urlar* of the city's song. I wanted the grace notes. It was an hour to get there and as the bus stopped and started, I thought of how I saw an otter once, at the river. I thought of wild garlic and brambles and tumbled several seasons into one. I got off by the police station and walked to the crest of a hill where a church is and saw in one deep-set window St Bride with St Modwenna, and this other woman in scant outline squeezed off to the side: Sister Dara. I took a picture. And then I walked down to the river. But it felt like a re-enactment. With no otter. I sat riverside (and I'm not going to rhyme that with 'cried'). On the way home, but not yet out of Musselburgh (The Honest Toun), a high man walked in front of the bus, the bus stopped suddenly, and a woman slid off her seat and right down the middle aisle. The high man wasn't hurt, just high, but he said he wanted to die. We sat there waiting for the police to come and I thought about St Bride. And what about Sister Dara sort of expiring at the edge of everything. I took out my phone and looked at their faces. I started to research. Sister Dara was a blind nun who, when her sight was restored by St Bride, didn't want it. She asked to be returned to the beauty of darkness.

Already there

One day Tamara surprised and delighted me by turning up at my door. It was December and about to be my fourth Christmas in Edinburgh. I had been missing my children, and when I heard Tamara's voice through the buzzer, I flew down the stairs to meet them. We rented a car and drove into the Highlands. One day we were staying just out of Aviemore, and Tamara had decided to go skiing, so I drove to the Cairngorm Reindeer Centre in Glenmore Forest Park to take a guided tour. About ten of us walked up and up into a very high field, and there they were – these elegant, antler-balancing creatures floating across the snow on their snowshoe hooves. Some ate from our hands, their antlers like small, sudden winter trees in front of us, while in every direction unfolded the white Cairngorms, the reindeers' free-ranging home.

After the tour, there was time to fill before picking up Tamara, so I wandered into the Glenmore Forest Park Visitors Centre where I found an ordnance survey map for Badenoch and Upper Strathspey. I knew from my reading that the Davidson clan (the other side of my Scottish family) originally hailed from Badenoch, so I was excited to find the map and asked the shop assistant if Badenoch was close by. I knew it was mountainous. I knew it was one of the most interior parts of Scotland. He took my money, handed me back the map and said, *It's here. This place.* I went into the café, ordered coffee and a scone and opened out the map. Not only was I already there, but in 2016 when I'd stayed at Inshriach Bothy by the River Spey on a writing residency, I was already there. And the day before, when Tamara and I walked around Loch an Eilein and I said, with surprise, *I think this is the loch I walked to when I stayed at Inshriach Bothy*, I was already there. And when I fell over on the ice on the Loch an Eilein walk, I was already there.

And when a nice young man and Tamara pulled me to my feet and dusted me off, and I walked along holding my arm, and Tamara pointed to the island in the middle of the loch and said, *There's the castle*, because we'd been looking in vain for the castle on the island, I was already there. And when I said *Maybe it only appears when you need it*, and we laughed, we were already there.

Diary June 2019

On an EasyJet flight from Edinburgh to Berlin the young man beside me was reading the score for Jonathan Dove's *The Passing of the Year*, a song cycle for double chorus, two pianos and percussion. He was conducting as he read. He was wearing shorts, a T-shirt and jandals and had a thick beard. The creamy pages strung with notes lay open on his broad lap. His hands swam in the currents of the music. I tried not to move, in case he stopped doing what he was doing. I just turned my eyes towards him and watched. The piece opens with an invocation:

Oh earth re-turn Oh earth re-turn Oh earth re-turn Oh earth re-turn
Oh earth re-turn Oh earth re-turn Oh earth re-turn Oh earth re-turn
Oh earth re-turn Oh earth re-turn Oh earth re-turn Oh earth re-turn

The music dips and rises and then holds still in the air. He held it there with his fingertips, so he and I and the notes, the double chorus, the two pianos and the percussion were suddenly paused, a single kestrel hovering in place with the opal earth laid out beneath it, until with a swoop it freed us to run back into the thickets of ourselves.

The photography exhibition

In Barcelona, the trip a 60th birthday present from Elliot, I went to the same tiny restaurant every day. I liked how it was open to the street. I squeezed bright, sharp lime juice over couscous and sipped my tall glass of cava.

On my last day, too late to catch up with all the things I'd failed to see, I felt a familiar shame. I felt as though I were walking with a hook under my sternum, pulling me forward. I remembered that I didn't know how to live, how I never had, not for one moment. I was a teenager again and the grinning bus driver was calling down the bus telling me to *Smile!* My ridiculous hair curling in every direction. My burning. How do I make this story when I haven't managed to maintain the structures and relationships that punctuate and shape a life, when several of the waymarks are missing – Picasso, Miró, marriage, house. I hadn't made it into the Sagrada Familia, *the sacred family*, the unfinished bone-dance building. As I walked through the city I felt as though I were swimming into empty spaces, the way my diver son in dark, muscular water throws light ahead of himself with his torch and swims towards it. Then, as if following behind my son, I saw something that might have been waiting for me. At the Ajuntament Building in Plaça Sant Jaume there was a flyer for a photography exhibition – August Sander's *People of the Twentieth Century*. The flyer had a photograph of four serious young people, intellectuals, who seemed to look at me. The building was beautiful – airy and lofty – and there were no lines of people waiting to get in. My heart lifted. I stumbled up the cool stone stairs; I stumbled back into my body, my purposeful body.

Sander's *People of the Twentieth Century* is a huge and legendary archive of portraits of German society from 1910 to the mid 1950s; from the Weimar Republic to the Second World War and the repercussions of Nazism. The photographs are modern prints on the base of the original gelatin silver negative glass plate. They have such depth to them. They are unsentimental and politically incisive, the blurb says. They are very human. I stood a long time in front of the photograph that had been on the flyer, the one that had caught my eye. It was called *Proletarian Intellectuals* – with three young men and one woman who was wearing an enviable beret. They looked serious to the point of burdened, but they were sitting close together with one standing behind, leaning over the others in a way that a friend would get in close with friends. Their chins were tilted down and their eyes lifted up, as though the photographer was standing above them. I moved through the rooms but kept returning to those four.

Back in my hotel room I discovered that the woman in the photograph was Else Lasker-Schüler, a German Jewish poet, essayist and playwright. I found an article about Else in *Deutsche Welle* that told me she was considered to be Germany's most important female Expressionist poet. Born in 1869, she lived an unconventional Bohemian life in Berlin. I sat looking at the word 'Bohemian' for a moment, wondering what it actually meant, then carried on reading with the words *Bohemian* and *unconventional* cooling on my tongue.* Else was very poor and she lived with friends, or sometimes in cheap hotels, and, the article said, she sometimes lived on the street. She dressed extravagantly and called herself marvellous names, like Prince Jussuf of Thebes or Blue Jaguar or Tino of Baghdad. She wrote a collection of letters to her husband about why she wanted to break up with him, and about the thrill of fresh love. She included these letters in a novel, written in a mix of poetry and

---

* Bohemia was once a kingdom in the Holy Roman Empire, then it was a province in the Austrian Habsburg Empire, and it is now a Central European country. It was wrongly believed to be the place where gypsies came from. Bohemian means moving in unconventional, artistic circles, which sometimes include uncertain settlement, or no settled home at all.

prose, called *Mein Herz*, or *My Heart*, 'A novel of love, with pictures and real, living people.' The German original had an additional subtitle: 'My heart – (belongs to) nobody.'

In 1932 Else fled Nazi Germany and lived out her life in Jerusalem, where she advocated for equal rights for homosexuals and for reconciliation between Jews and Arabs. She was stripped of her German citizenship in 1938. I found a poem of hers, 'My People', first published in her book *Hebrew Ballads*, 1959, in English translation in the 1969 *Jewish Quarterly* magazine, a London-based international magazine. Her poetry has been described as echoing the passion of *Song of Songs* and you can hear this echo here:

My People

It rots –
The rock from which I spring
And my Godsongs sing . . .
I plunge sheer down from the track
And babble quite on my own,
Fardown, alone over the wailing stone
Towards the sea.

I have
Gone flowing so beyond
The fermented sap
That is my blood.
Yet time and again
All my echoes respond
When ghostly, towards east,
My people
Rotting rockbones
Cry to God.

I am not surprised at her poem. Why wouldn't Else Lasker-Schüler aka Prince Jussuf of Thebes write something like this – so raw and brave. I am grateful for the compound word 'fardown' and for the poem's description of how one can go so far beyond blood and then cry out with blood-cries. I don't think it's true that her heart belonged to nobody. Our hearts are Bohemian, steeped in the colour and chaos and cost of what they love.

*

Before Barcelona I had been in New Zealand. Tamara's father, Bennett, had died very quickly from cancer. On the day that Elliot and I went to the crematorium to pick up Bennett's ashes, we left Tamara putting together a photo board for their dad's funeral.

His image, across his years on earth, was right there as we gathered to remember him on that searingly hot day on the grassy patch beside the sea at Pukerua Bay. On the board Bennett is sitting playing the piano with his dog on his lap, or he is pretending to let two-year-old Tamara push him in the buggy, a baby's bonnet on his head. Playing the fool, like his father. His father and mother would always arrive late, *Here we are, the late Friedmanns!* Laughter.

My sister, Clare, sang a song for Bennett, 'If I Had a Boat' by Lyle Lovett, and it just happened that it was his favourite song. She hadn't known that when she chose it, or it chose her. The photographs weren't quite across the years. They were across his New Zealand years, after he had migrated to New Zealand in the 70s with his then wife. This followed the nine months of military service that all white males in South Africa had to complete (Bennett, a pacifist, requested non-combative work). A German, French, Israeli, New Zealand friend of

Bennett's got up and talked about his European sensibility (his parents were born in Latvia) and his particular European sense of humour. I thought that perhaps he had helped her to feel less lonely here in the far south of the world. She read from the Mourner's Kaddish, tears on her face, under the bright bright sun. A breeze shot through, tipping over several wineglasses and breaking them.

The next day I was burnt from sitting outside at the beach service, despite sunblock and a wide-brimmed hat. The same wind that tipped the glasses tipped its brim and exposed me. The tattered ozone layer above New Zealand means that, with my Scottish skin, I burn quickly. I was burnt across half of my face; one half red, the other pale. I felt sick. Discombobulated, I said to my kids. We were sitting around the table at Bennett's house, and I was dabbing the burnt half of my face with the cooling ooze from an arm of aloe vera that grows like a giant anemone at the top of the drive. *Discombobulated* I said. Trying to magic up a funny, childhood word that might feel like a tiny balm in the presence of death, and that might soothe my grown child's grieving heart.

*

Perhaps the people in Sander's photographs knew that their portraits would go down in history. Or become memorials of people lost to a terrible history. The artists in the photographs might have thought that they would be remembered for the art they represented: their books, their music, their paintings, their sculptures. Or perhaps they knew that they could be lost to one history, and preserved in another. Perhaps the rural bride with the freckles wearing the halo of flowers, or the boxer in his shorts, or the office worker with their bag, would have known that they'd go down, as in be 'caught', in their histories because

Sander was catching them there. Sander standing in front of them with his camera. They, in front of Sander, with their lives.

At the photography exhibition in rooms that were as deep and still as a held breath, there was very little smiling. In the photographs the people looked out, and also in. They looked out to the world and also in to their lives. It was almost rhythmical, like breathing.

Emergence

My two grown kids climb a silver sand dune in Death Valley in the Mojave Desert. I look at them on the skyline. They look for a moment like herons, all flow and folded primaries and flights, heads bent, under the contractions of the sky.

Before the world changed, my kids and I flew into LAX: me from Scotland, Elliot from Australia, and Tamara from New Zealand. It was a journey a long time in the planning. It was January 2020. Our road trip took us into four states: inland from Los Angeles, California to Arizona, Utah, Nevada and back into California, driving from San Francisco to LA via the Pacific Coast Highway.

We mostly stayed in small towns and cheap motels. One night we stopped at an adobe cabin at Vermillion Cliffs in Northern Arizona, and in the morning, standing at the edge of the empty road cradling my tea, I looked across to the sandstone cliffs: the red spine of land made from drifting desert sand. We drove to a nearby bridge that spans the Colorado River Canyon where, holding our breath, we watched condors drift and fly and settle on high red ledges. We were almost alone, except that on the far side of the bridge there were three women behind trestle tables that shone with turquoise jewellery. Three condors glided over a vast emptiness above the river. We couldn't take our eyes off them. The gift of it, that a few at least were still here. We lookers and listeners, we flawed and porous beings, didn't know how imperilled *we* were about to be. Only eight weeks later, trapped in my flat, a month-long twitch in my right eye, a kind of erratic flight across a blue-green globe. The Colorado River Canyon, the Vermillion Cliffs, the catastrophe I didn't want to see. Our ongoing histories. Flick flick flick at the edge of my eye. A mental feathering. Fear.

My kids went back to the car, and I stopped to look at the jewellery, a trestle table two or three planks deep between me and one woman. Seeing me hesitate she reached out a hand. I pulled back. *My daughter needs clothes for school* she said, and still I walked away. As usual I didn't know how to contribute, or how not to contribute. How to live and how to live with myself. My kids said that's why they didn't look at the turquoise jewellery, because they didn't want to feel like I was feeling. In the car we drove towards the Grand Canyon, where nothing is relative.

A deep and unforgiving cold. Elliot wore the Fair Isle beanie I knitted him (the pattern is named for Tantallon Castle – still there, in ruins, opposite Bass Rock in North Berwick). The Grand Canyon was a believable heaven: the pastel pinks and mauves and blues, the cathedral shapes and mile-deep spaces. A blue jay. How profound the domestic moment became there in that vastness: passing hot coffee between us, from my hands to his, and his to theirs, between the bodies that first lived inside me. The Havasupai people live by the river at the bottom of the canyon, where they grow, among other wondrous things, peach trees. The blossoms from the peach trees drift from branches in a spring wind, up into the pale, sculpted spaces. American writer and poet Don Marquis said that publishing a collection of poetry was like dropping a rose petal down the Grand Canyon and waiting for the echo. Well here, once, on an updraft, a twitch of wind, a peach petal floating up, an echo of sorts.

After the deep cold of winter. The memory of pleasure. A collectivity of peach juice. The absolute potential of embodiment.

Eight months alone in my flat

I bought an ironing board – partly to have a good surface on which to iron my Scottish grandmother's lacework tablecloth, and partly because I wanted to run my hand across its recently worked, warm surface because then it feels like an animal – a horse or a dog or a deer – patiently bearing my hand. You see, I missed fellow beating hearts, and all their complex bloodwork.

*

I sent Elliot a book called *The Soul of an Octopus*, and Tamara sent me a book called *The Song of Trees*. This is one way in which we love each other.

*

Once in New Zealand, when I was sitting outside at a pub in Wellington feeling a bit broken by family fracture, a famous New Zealand poet who had a Scottish mother sat beside me and sang this song:

My heart's in the Highlands, my heart is not here.
My heart's in the Highlands, a-chasing the deer.

Buttoning their coats

Diary

10/10/2020

I have been talking with ghosts for eight months. Alone in my flat but for my ancestors, and even they are buttoning up their coats these days. There is a second wave of Covid, and I can't do any more months on my own. The kids think I should go home. My friends think I should go home. I know I should go home. I know it's time to un-make the egg I built with me inside it. My stone egg in its stone nest in the tenement-tree in this stone-and-air city.

11/10/2020

Because of lockdown, I haven't seen the pink-footed geese arrive from Iceland into the Aberlady Reserve this year. It is a small tradition for me, only a few years old, but still, not to see them is hard. No geese cacophony, no wings creaking overhead through the quick dusk. No sunset orange glint on mudflats. Different things are flying overhead, different things are disturbing the air. After a broken sleep yesterday, I got up early to walk in Holyrood Park – I saw my trees; they said Go with a whole heart *and* Come back with a whole heart, *and then I saw the pink-footed geese fly overhead in a big raggedy skein.*

12/10/2020

Joy had a five-hour operation on her leg to take out the cancer. It's hard to think of my very petite 'big' sister going through this. Melbourne feels a long way away right now. But even if I were there, I couldn't visit her. Before the operation, we, her family, had a Zoom dance party for her across three countries, two hemispheres.

Later, Elliot and I Zoomed and to begin with we just sat looking at each other. Where do you start?

Elliot & Ret sent me pics. They are shifting into their new home. They look so happy, and behind them, in the garage, there is a highchair. I bought a suitcase. Checked my tickets. Clocks here went back. It is dark so early.

13/10/2020

Took two jackets to a tailor to get the sleeves shortened. I am doing this great preparation like a Victorian woman going on a long journey.

I told Adult Education, Open Book, and my adult literacy creative writing group that I'm leaving. Then I began to talk with a friend on Zoom and got a migraine and had to go to bed. It's been more years than I can remember since I had a migraine. It is hard to leave my hard-won and beloved work. This country where I found myself.

3/11/2020 (my last day in Edinburgh):

Yesterday afternoon I was lying on the couch staring out the window (I am good at this after eight months of practice), and a kestrel landed on the window ledge and looked at me. Its heavy upright body, the oiled turn of its head, the glossy and utterly focused predator eyes. I have had seagulls and pigeons, so many seagulls and pigeons, land on the window ledge, but never a falcon. I have never been looked at in such a way. I have watched kestrels hover in the air in Holyrood Park at dusk, hunting for prey. But never this dense gold-brown body on the other side of the pane. There have been huge full moons lately. Autumnal harvest moons. I went up to my trees. A group of them in long coats stood waiting at a crowded dock. A message from the ancestors. A kind of performance. A quiet farewell from people who know about farewells. I looked and looked and looked, and then they went away.

My last night in Edinburgh

I arranged tealights on a china plate and set it on the floor in the centre of the empty living room. Outside it was dark already, night dropping earlier and earlier now that autumn had arrived. The rows of tenement chimneys from across the way, visible from my windows, were inside the dark, as was the verdigris cupola of Old College, University of Edinburgh on South Bridge. The cross from St Patrick's Church with its perching seagulls was inside the dark. The crags with their crows were in the dark. The junkies and drinkers were inside the dark – the only people still outside in the plague town. Courtyards with their bins and shrubs and stone walls were inside the dark. The Writer's Museum with Robert Burns's desk inside it was locked up and in the dark. The jutting clock face from the Canongate Tolbooth dissolved into the dark as did the Netherbow Bell. The barely-there etched poems on the Storytelling Centre windows were rubbed out by the dark. The castle and the hard volcanic rock it stands on, all inside the dark. The dark flowed like a river down the Royal Mile from the castle to the palace, through tributaries of narrow closes where it washed up against stone faces. The undressed cherry trees outside the Canongate Kirk, all in the dark, and the poet Robert Fergusson who walked and walked was in the dark again. Holyrood Parliament – hard to imagine that *one* window was not lit with somebody working – but no. Holyrood was in the dark.

Jane and Jules arrived at my building, and I buzzed them in. Jane and I are both members of *12*, the collective of women writers, and Jules is an artist who lived in the Canongate just down the road from me. I had met Jules when she did some paintings springing from poems in my collection *Islander*, which became part of her exhibition, *Of Wild Kin*. The exhibition included responses to the work of several Scottish poets, including Jane. We read the poems at the exhibition opening in the Scottish Poetry Library just a few days before the first lockdown. One poet, Lydia Harris, had flown in from her home in Orkney to read. It was a charged night, on the cusp of a strange new life. The display of our books for the opening sat in the window of the closed poetry library for months, and I would sometimes turn off at Crichton's Close to walk past them on my way to Holyrood Park.

Earlier in the day, Jules and I had taken a load of stuff from my flat to one of the few charity shops that were still open, and then she asked me if there was somewhere particular that I would like to go, and we drove to a favourite spot by the River Esk in Musselburgh – the river that had held me when I was unhappily working at Tesco, and in which, one miraculous day, I watched an otter play. The dusk fell and shifted colours, the river turned from blue to a metallic grey then softened into charcoal, and above our heads a cloud of pipistrels flickered through branches. I had chosen this place to light a candle for my Scottish grandparents soon after my arrival in Scotland. I had sat a tealight candle in a pāua shell found on the south coast of Wellington, where they had lived, and partly filled the shell with water from the river. I had lit the candle and thought of my grandfather's songs and my grandmother's stories, then blew out the candle and tipped the water back into the river, by way of returning them to Scotland, where they began.

In my flat, we sat with our backs against cushions, talking. The little lights flickered. Jane wrestled with the cork in the Moët. It popped and flew and we laughed. It was hard to say goodbye to these friends. We'd shared our work, collaborated, and cheered each other on. We'd been strong women in our 50s and then, Jane and I, our 60s, together. I didn't want this degree of living and manifesting to stop. But the truth was that in eight months of lockdown I had met up with friends, in the flesh, maybe six times. And I was going home to my children and (at that time) a Covid-free country with the impressive Prime Minister Jacinda Ardern handling the crisis so well, and what a blessing to be doing that. But still, despite those truths, something deep inside my heart was breaking. My friends left, and I sat up in the company of tealight candles. And then I blew them out, and like the chimneys and the clockface and the tollbooth, I was also inside the dark.

Five

These islands

Jack and the old gods

In Edinburgh Airport the few people waiting for flights sat with their bags between their feet or wandered around with a punch-drunk look. I was flying to London, the first stop on my way to New Zealand. On that same day, London was shutting down because of the second wave of Covid. I went to an empty, dimly lit airport café, and when the shop assistant finally appeared, ordered a coffee. I sat down, opened a book and didn't read it. After a while a man came into the café. He wandered up to the counter where the shop assistant wasn't – she seemed to materialise and dematerialise, and neither of us could see where she might have gone. The man, who looked like a businessman in his late 40s, was wearing an expensive suit and, in the world we had just lost, could be perceived to have some power. He stood at the counter with his hands hanging down. There was no sharp ringing of a bell to alert the café worker, no brisk *Hello?* to get her attention. The young woman didn't come, and after a while the man drifted back into the lounges and walkways of the quiet, crepuscular airport.

London airport was busier than Edinburgh, of course, but still quiet and eerie. I stayed the night at a deserted, nearby hotel (a porter popped his head out of the hotel door to see me arriving with my bags and disappeared again without offering me any help). I sucked my fabric mask into and out of my mouth as I pulled my two suitcases behind me. The man at reception was behind a Perspex shield and couldn't hear me speak (my quiet voice, the mask, the Perspex), so I walked to the edge of the shield and talked to him – so stupid really, but we were both tired. After I had checked in, I stood in front of the lift – it was a small, narrow, kind of dark-brown hotel, and the lift too was narrow and dark brown – and I couldn't step into it. I breathed hotly into my mask and felt a cramping in my chest. It was only one floor, but I couldn't make myself do it. The woman working at the empty bar beside the lifts began watching me with concern on her face. I went back to the man at reception and told him I was feeling claustrophobic and couldn't get in the lift. He was kind and it was no trouble, he wheeled my bags into the lift. I walked up the stairs to my room, and the woman behind the bar watched me with a kind of pity.

I hoped I would get away. I hoped I wouldn't get stuck in a locked-down London. I especially hoped I wouldn't get stuck in the empty, dark-brown hotel with its porter, Hitchcock like, doing the briefest of cameos. I looked searchingly out of the window, as if it would be possible for me to see if I'd be able to leave tomorrow. I looked towards all the compass points as though reading the weather. I checked and re-checked that I had my passport, my ticket, and my Managed Isolation Allocation Voucher for New Zealand, without which I wouldn't be allowed on the plane. Then I lay down on the bed. I didn't want to eat my dinner in the empty dining room that bled into the reception area and the bar with the pitying woman. It was all I could do to hold onto the small buoyancy that was keeping full-blown panic at bay. I wanted to say to someone *If this wasn't so horrible it would be funny.* But there was no one to say things to. Except my children who didn't need me adding to the concerns they already had as they waited for me on the other side of the world, and friends who were either in the UK dealing with lockdown, or in New Zealand and whom I hadn't seen for ages. As for so many others, the pandemic was pushing me hard against my life, its shape, my choices. It wasn't just loneliness I was feeling, it was the essential oil of loneliness, extracted and bottled and sitting on the arc of a floating rib, on the heart side. I paid £10 to have my dinner carried to my first-floor room.

The next morning, I got away. In Singapore all of the staff wore PPE. As we walked into the airport terminal our temperatures were taken with a blue thermometer that was held up to our foreheads. There was a ten-hour wait at Singapore, and I had stupidly imagined going to the airport's butterfly enclosure and having a swim, as though a different country was a whole different planet. Most of the airport was closed off. We couldn't go more than a few yards from the door we walked in through. I lay down on one of the loungers by the window and, mercifully and surprisingly, slept.

One upside of the hairy business of flying at that time was having a whole row of seats to myself. I pushed up the armrests and lay along the seats on each of the two long-haul flights. I was tearful at times, nothing dramatic, just quiet tears dripping onto the seat my face was pressed against. It wasn't about leaving Scotland, well, it was but not entirely. It was a wider, more overarching sadness for us all, we humans, and how much we've messed things up. There was also a letting go in those tears, the kind of deep letting go one does when one has been in danger for a long time and is almost home. In the spaces during the flight when I was upright and more collected, I read Marilynne Robinson's *Jack*, the fourth book in the Gilead sequence, and it took me back into the world of Gilead: a place I was very grateful, especially at that moment, to return to.

Jack is set in 1950s Missouri. Jack is the son of a gentle preacher from Gilead, Iowa, and one of two sons in a family of six siblings. He is a troubling and troubled child. His family love him dearly, and he them, but he cannot live the life they hoped for him. He cannot be other than himself: original, playful, poetic and struggling to maintain the boundaries between mine and thine. After hurting some people badly, he makes a vow to do no harm, while living a life as a self-described bum. Then, in the segregated city of St Louis, Missouri he falls in love with an African American woman, Della, a schoolteacher and the daughter of a distinguished Memphis family – her father is a Bishop in a Black Church and ambitious for his daughter to take part in the work of claiming a rightful place in society. But Della falls in love with Jack.

Neither Memphis nor Gilead can provide a safe spiritual, emotional and physical home for Jack and Della. When Jack tells Della that, although he knows he shouldn't visit her, sitting with her on the stoop of her house in the dark calms him, she says, 'It's real. That peace.'

The book is about seeing and being seen. Jack and Della illuminate each other, even when they are only able to snatch moments in the dark. In his relationship with Della, the difficulties Jack has had distinguishing between mine and thine are a gift. Human-made binaries are dissolved for the sake of something better: 'He and Della had been there, in that luminous absence of distinctions, in that radiant night.'

After reading *Jack*, I pick up the other book, the other talisman I had brought with me for the flight: *Margaret Tait: Poems, Stories and Writings*. Tait was born on Orkney in 1918. She was educated in Edinburgh, studied medicine and served in India, Sri Lanka and Malaya in the Royal Army Medical Corps. After studying filmmaking in Rome in the early 50s, she returned to Edinburgh, to a flat in Rose Street, where she ran the Rose Street Film Festivals. Feeling some frustration with what she felt was the 'sameness' of the Scottish filmmaking scene at that time, she worked independently, establishing her own film company, Ancona Films, and, in 1968 returned to live and work on Orkney. Tait was a pioneering filmmaker who played with language and the concept of reality, in her films and in her poetry. Ali Smith writes in the introduction to the book that Tait was interested in the concept of time, and the 'making-new she perceived as the heartbeat of the poetic act.' Then she quotes Tait, 'Each new moment is a new moment.'

The line that Smith quotes comes from a poem called 'By the Book' from Tait's 1960 poetry collection *The Hen and the Bees*, where she writes among other things of the 'old gods'. She rejects the idea of the Bible being the last word on how to live (the question Jack wrestles with so painfully in *Jack*). She asks, 'How could it possibly be that someone else's / revelation / Is more to go by / Than the inner revelation of oneself to oneself?' She is asking us, in the poem, to think about fluidity and time and change.

In her poem 'Other Gods, Other Ways', Tait writes about the fallible old gods who, rather than being worshipped, were enjoyed as 'superior friends'. A concept in stark contrast, I imagine, to any possible relationship with the harsh Presbyterian God that generations of Scots grew up with. The first part of the poem talks about how that God 'Got us all in such a muddle that we no longer know who we are'. And then she writes about the old northern gods, the 'superior friends', and the poem then releases itself from even the long-ago time of those northern gods, saying at the end that there was 'something away beyond them again'.

What stays with me most strongly from the poem is a description of the old gods 'casually' regarding the building of the stone circles on Orkney. The old gods come and go like relatives. They have their own lives to be getting on with. They are turning their faces, briefly, to gigantic human endeavour, and this brief look lights up the face of the stones. The scene feels to me both relaxed and monumental. I don't know if this is how it was, or how it felt for those long-ago people who built the Ring of Brodgar at the far edge of the Neolithic period, whether they felt the gods to be casual visitors and superior friends or not. I'm thinking maybe not. But the poem draws on a sense, a kind of ancestral memory, a time when the spiritual and physical community was not yet riven.

Managed Isolation at the Novotel in Auckland was efficient and prison-like. I couldn't open a window in my room and had to take a lift and give my name and room number before I could do my circular, socially distanced walk around the carpark (no sitting, no running). Families with small children got pavement chalk and had the central part of the carpark for drawing on. We all looked at the drawings as we walked round and round. There were stick figures, hopscotch, big sums that the children could step through as well as calculate, there were elaborate roads for toy cars, there were aliens and superheroes. Parents and children bent over their work. We were back in the 70s, and there was something sweet about it. Except that parents reminded children not to go near anyone, and especially not to touch anyone. And except that there were police, security, army and every variety of uniformed person watching us all the time. Not bullying, and sometimes friendly, but just disconcertingly there. One day, desperate to see a bigger view than the one I could see from my window, I left my room with an idea of reaching the picture window at the end of the hallway. I realised I was asking for trouble and, sure enough, halfway down the hallway a big man in military fatigues suddenly appeared in front of me and asked, *Are you lost, ma'am?* I understood the message and went back to my room. I couldn't read, I couldn't write, I was like a patient who is too unwell to do anything except what they are told. In some ways I felt as though I were still in the dark-brown hotel in London, except I couldn't take the stairs. A notice on the door to the stairwell said that if anyone used the stairs the police would be called.

In the room opposite mine were a couple with two young children. The mother and I often opened our doors at the same time to pick up our paper bags of food. We bent over our bags as if in a deep bow to each other. I saw her smooth brown hair, its tidy parting. One day I saw her hand swish a little bare-arsed kid back into the room. We were masked and business-like and anxious; it was over a week before, on straightening up, we paused to catch each other's eye and say hello, our eyes lighting each other up. It was a look, a moment, that had in it a shared hope for a good outcome. *Della says to Jack, 'I want you to be alive. That's all. Nothing complicated.'*

These islands

I sit on the shore
recovering from this

long breath-held dive to get here.
The shudder of relief
to breathe in air.

Such air in this place   the river of wind
between   these islands
lands
here and   here and
here

Less breathing in

material

Less breathing in material.

How to measure land-loss against
the gentle constant of breath.

I have left Scotland – the word, the place –
the way we move through each other like light through water.

Infrastructure will not solve distance.
Nor can you build a country inside another country.

However – a word that sounds like a river of wind
between islands – *however*

the word *bridge*, its excavating consonants,
its failing reach,
sits deep in the gullies of my mouth.

Wellington peonies

December 2020

There are gushy peonies outside the florists' door.
Don't you just want to push your face into them? the florist says
which is a kindness because
I am already pushing my face into them.

So petalled. So inhabited. So pink. And
bunched together in a zinc bucket like something
cheaper, less luscious, more ordinary.

Mrs Dalloway said she would buy the flowers herself.
Netted by light and breathing rivery London air. Oh
to blossom into invisibility! To walk through the uncanny
narrow glade between buildings, that sudden temperature drop.
To see people in long coats at the bus stop undulate
in late spring wind, like kelp forests.

Bliss. Katherine Mansfield has Bertha arrange green and
    purple grapes
on a long, glossy table. Bertha is in a sudden ecstasy for a life
she is about to lose. Of course, she doesn't know it yet. She
    thinks only that
the purple grapes bring the carpet up to the table.

Divorce, violence, and violets

The persistent nor'westerly shrieked, and my hilltop Wellington Airbnb felt very 'airy' and fragile as the weatherboards creaked and shook. I was in bed and still searching my computer for Vida. I discovered a piece in the 11 February 1941 issue of the *Aberdeen Press and Journal*, headed 'Bieldside Divorce', where Vida wins a decree of divorce against her husband Henry on the grounds of cruelty. The shock of seeing it written on the page was tempered by a small bolt of gratitude for an honest use of language – I'd found out some things about Henry's violence. I closed my computer and tucked down further into bed where the slippery, shiny red quilt did nothing to keep the cold out.

The next morning the wind dropped, and I took a bus to Kelburn. A student I was mentoring had offered me her house while she and her husband were in Auckland welcoming their new grandchild into the world. I was going to have a look around the house and be shown where things were. It was a generous and welcome offer. The house was beautiful, with wood panelling and deep windows looking out onto a garden dense and shimmery under a soft rain. There were drawings and paintings by John Drawbridge, Russell Drysdale, Robin White. I stood in the house relishing its quiet, its solid roof, its beauty, the bookcases full of Aotearoa New Zealand and Pasifika books. My friend made tea which we drank in the TV room, where photos of children and grandchildren were dotted between books and paintings. I relished the thought of two weeks in that house, but an awkward feeling came. My friend who I hardly knew, and her husband who I didn't know at all, were letting me stay in their home with a home's vaults of deep privacy.

I struggle to receive favours with any sort of comfort, and thought this was a failing in me that ran in co-dependent parallel with my tendency towards over-politeness (which can end up seeming rude), until I read this in Rachel Cusk's *Coventry*, in an essay on her separation from her husband: 'Help is dangerous because it exists outside the human economy: the only payment for help is gratitude.' That sentence, on first reading, sang out to me in multiple harmonies worthy of the Mormon Tabernacle Choir. Help can feel tangling, as though the balance of the relationship has tipped. And yet, and yet, I *was* very grateful to be helped. And doesn't help keep the wheels turning in this difficult, divide-and-conquer human world? And while help *is* dangerous, in the way that Cusk points out, could we turn ourselves slightly differently towards the help, understanding it as part of the knitting together of community, could we think – *could I think* – differently about it? I took a breath, trying to access this less difficult possibility that my friend and I were helping each other; that help is kept live, radically live, by being passed along. But then I thought of my recent home, rented but my own, my fourth-floor Edinburgh flat, and something flew into my side with a sharp twinge, leaving a feeling of bareness. I had lost the space I made for myself in Edinburgh.

My friend showed me her garden, and we breathed in its different delicate scents. I followed behind her, exhausted by feeling at-home and homeless and homesick all at once.

I shifted into the Kelburn house. There were clouds of heart-shaped violet leaves in the garden, and I couldn't resist parting them to look for flowers even though they are a late-winter and early-spring bloom, and it was summer. I thought about how many single violets I have picked and placed in a tiny glass bottle on the edge of a windowsill or the centre of a table in a multitude of baches and cottages in this country. How I have stood looking at the single violet, or leaned towards it to smell its high, dry, sweet, ethereal scent which is there and then isn't. The scent disappears as if by magic, but it's not magic – there's a compound called ionone which gives violets their scent but also, after a few moments, shuts the scent receptors down. You need to turn your head away and then back to enjoy the scent again.

I felt a rush of exhaustion and impatience at myself when I told people how lucky I felt to be back, when really I was unmoored, missing the landscape of Scotland, and worrying about my friends. It annoyed me slightly, all the conversation about the luck of being here, the humorous Twitter hashtag 'Hellhole' with its gorgeous photos of New Zealand. I felt sad and tired and bad tempered. I realised it was unreasonable to be irritated when I had escaped the horrors of the virus and the potential terrifying scenario of being unable to breathe, all alone, 12,000 miles from the people who loved me best. But it reminded me of other times when being protected from life's dangers and thus potentials made me feel desperate. I knew that this virus, its breath-taking worldwide disruption, could not be compared to parts of my life – it resists metaphor and simile – but the requirement to stay home to be safe *could* shake up oppressive memories and set them walking.

When I was 24, pregnant and nauseous, and somewhat unexpectedly living deep in the country, I found some respite from complicated feelings by building a herb garden. Kester and I had not long shifted from our home close to Wellington to the isolated rural North Taranaki. Kester was working long hours, and I was looking for an anchor point, something to hold me in this unfamiliar place. I'd left behind a herb garden, and I would make another one. I would make a small, fragrant place that was mine, inside the unfolding countryside with its naked paddocks, its shelter belts of rustling eucalyptus, its milk trucks and the cold breath from Mt Taranaki. My mother, who was visiting, stood watching me dig and plant as the wind whipped across fields and wrapped itself around us. The wind kept blowing my long hair into my face and my hands were covered in dirt; I asked Mum to move the tentacle of hair that had drifted into my mouth, and she did. Then she stood there, hugging her beige jacket around her, watching me plant sage and rosemary, mint and marjoram, feverfew and tansy, borage and lavender, vervain and violets. Like the binary that produces the Madonna or whore roles for women, another binary allows for women to be sorted along botanical lines: the arranger of flowers or the gatherer of herbs. Women have always arranged flowers: in the church, in the house, for weddings, for funerals. With their wide-open faces, their colours, their on-display sex organs, their pollen, their beauty, their scent, and the cut-ness of their stems, flowers are traditionally women's work. *Mrs Dalloway said she would buy the flowers herself.* It is a strange moment of namelessness (Mrs somebody) and agency. It is the walk, of course, that is important. It is being out in the beautiful, regretful, dangerous world. Buying the flowers is Mrs Dalloway's portal on that beautiful London morning in 1923 into the world, a world in which she will quickly become Clarissa. On the day that I was building the herb garden, when my hair drifted into my mouth, I was also doing some urgent work outside the house. My mother, who loved me, stood there in the wind, holding the line between womanliness and witchcraft – holding it, and holding me, calling me back, asking if I was cold, meaning *I am cold standing here watching you.* Asking if I wanted to go inside, meaning *I want you to come inside with me.*

Mrs Dalloway steps outside her house, where she is preparing to host a party, giving the reason that she is going to buy the flowers *herself.* Although she is using the currency of upper-class wife who must personally view the flowers that will decorate her party, it seems to me that she is using the power available to her, the undisputed territory of flowers, to get out of the house so that she can, for a moment, in that sunny mid-June day between the wars, become Clarissa. Call it a spell. Call it an uncovering (the cut flowers lifting away to reveal the rooted ones, *herself*).

The great lie visited upon women is that the world is dangerous and it's safer to stay home. That has not been my experience. When the world really is dangerous, as when there is a rapidly spreading and mutating virus, we go inside, all of us, because it is actually dangerous out there. There is no gender divide to this danger, it doesn't just get women, we all have to be inside. When women across the world are forced or frightened into staying inside for their own safety, what, or who, are women being protected from? The others of us (men), who also go home at some point? There is no logic to it, except the logic of oppression. And what about those who don't fit into the gender divide. Is a non-binary person safe to be outside? Are they safer inside? It's a ridiculous question.

I have been called a shrinking violet, but it's not true. I love the beautiful, regretful, dangerous world. I like being out in it. It suits me.

Once, on a cold, frosty pre-Christmas night in Edinburgh, I caught the bus to a course I was taking on witchcraft called *Toil and Trouble*, run by writers and witches Alice Tarbuck and Claire Askew. I loved the frosty Christmassy night, my warm coat, the bus ride down from Princes Street into Stockbridge with its ancient and quiet atmosphere through which the Water of Leith sang old songs. There was an excited hum in the room. We were going to make charms. The long table was covered in the fragrant green and silver of moss and sage and rosemary, birch and hawthorn, clusters of cloves and nutmeg, and bright-coloured thread to bind them together. We made charms to ward off fear or illness or lostness, for protection, to enhance love and belonging. We made charms for our children, our friends, our lovers, ourselves. We focused on our intentions and hopes as we bound the small, fragrant bundles with thread. When we had finished and cleared the table, we put our charms in front of us and made a charging spell, to bring them to life. Thirteen of us stood holding hands around the table, then drummed our feet while repeating a chant. It was powerful and exciting. Exciting to claim and name those things we have never stopped knowing about – intuition, connection, our relationship with the non-human world, and the power of language – and call it spell. A dynamic alternative to the divide and conquer story of scarcity that saps and ruins us.

In her beautiful book *A Spell in the Wild: A Year (and Six Centuries) of Magic* Alice Tarbuck writes that witches 'exist partially outside, and partially in response to, political systems and contemporary cultures.' She goes on:

> . . . the witch has an important role to play in imagining a fairer society, and in asking difficult questions of our current society. Witches can offer the world meaningful alternatives: alternative value systems, beliefs, and means of operating in the world. These are important regardless of whether or not the witch attends protests. To live in relation to a power that exists outside of our normal relations is to understand the world and its systems differently.

On the first night of *Toil and Trouble*, when we gathered around the long table, I looked at some of the young women in fabulous 'witchy' dresses and makeup and listened to the talk about ceremonies I'd never heard of, such as hand-fastings. I felt like the new girl at school. I felt that perhaps this wasn't what I'd been looking for. I wanted something scholarly, I thought, something quieter. Something more about paper and less about bodies! But being a witch is absolutely an experience of embodiment. And embodiment means connection.

I stepped back into my body when I planted herbs into the ground that Kester had prepared for me, in a circle as I'd asked, and not far from the house. Despite Taranaki's mountain, and its powerful, wild shoreline, I found the farming landscape of scraped-back earth, pregnant cows, thundering milk trucks and roadkill terrible to live amongst. I felt that the land didn't want me there, and when I think of its history, why should it? There are places where you can be your best self, where you can be useful, and there are places where you flounder. I floundered in Taranaki. I was not my best self. Almost without knowing, but really knowing exactly, I called on the herbs to protect me, to look after my pregnancy, to ground me, to find me. The only way back into form at that time was through getting outside and tending to the actual world. Alice writes:

> We must learn the cry of the world, and how to join it ethically, and to challenge its oppressions through our work. And we must learn, too, to ask for help when we need it.

Along with the announcement of Vida's divorce on the grounds of cruelty, I found two other entries that named Vida in the *Aberdeen Press and Journal*. On 25 May 1922, Vida, who would have been 12, is named as taking part in a production of *Sleeping Beauty*. Madame Isabel Murray's Dance School had put on a performance of the 'old ever-new tale from Grimm', that, the article says, is designed to 'delight "grown-ups" as well as young people in the audience'. We are told that the King was dressed in purple, and the Queen wore 'a dazzling dress of sunlight gold'. There are fairies in shimmering silver and 'flimsy violet chiffon.' It is described as a brilliant spectacle.

I can't resist doing some research into Madame Isabel Murray and find that she was a well-known dancer and dance teacher in Aberdeen who supplemented her income by fitting corsetry and also by teaching rifle skills at a shooting gallery in her home. Making a living in the arts has never been a straightforward affair.

Just over six years after the piece about *Sleeping Beauty*, there is another article that mentions Vida. It is about Henry and Vida's wedding that had taken place the day before, on 4 June 1928, Vida's 19th birthday. It includes an ornate description of Vida's wedding dress. The colour of the bridesmaids' dresses is love-in-a-mist blue, and they carried bouquets of sweet peas. Vida carried a bouquet of pink carnations, and her veil was held in place by a lover's knot of orange blossom.

Vida speaks

I, Vida, have this parallel life where I am combing my child's hair or laying a table. Where I am walking into my living room carrying flowers. Where I am like Chris in *Sunset Song* and despite everything – fathers, husbands, wars – I am able. I am good, like a deep lochen, pool, linn. Lucid. You can see right through me to my bedrock. I feed one child and dress another. Tell them stories. Laugh at their jokes. Walk into the hills with friends. A good life, instead of this one where I open my mouth and crows fly out. Here language climbs the walls and turns things inside about. Here, in this place, the Aberdeenshire seasons come visiting, but not properly. They come like anxious, embarrassed relatives, bag over arm, ready to leave at any moment. My sister writes to me, and I respond. When I can. We liked boys and clothes and parties. Books. So. We stay with versions of those topics. Never our children. Never the ways we didn't fit and couldn't do it. All the things we could and couldn't. How she managed. How I didn't. I open my mouth and crows fly out.

1928 Island Bay

It's late morning on a bright summer's day in Island Bay. My grandmother leaves her house at 39 Derwent Street, pushing my father in a large black pram and with his big brother, John, on a white rein. They walk around the corner from their house to The Parade and down towards the chemist. Shadows pour behind them as they walk. My grandmother looks at the pōhutukawa trees that line the street, the round red flowers still holding their soft spiny selves together. Later in summer they will drift apart and turn footpaths and gutters red, they will fall on hats and heads and shoulders. But today the summer has a spring-like gush to it and every new thing is full of the moment of perfect display, as though this holding could last.

My grandmother wears a forest green dress with a simple shallow scoop neckline, and on the right side below the neckline she wears a brooch, a silver thistle. My grandmother opens the door to the chemist and an older man, the owner, hurries to help her through. She tries not to bump the pram and gives the old man a smile, which is good payment, she thinks. Stuart is behind the counter, and his serious face brightens to see his sister and nephews. She, my grandmother, as usual wonders what goes on in Stuart's head; he doesn't give much away. But they are always pleased to be in the company of each other. The old man makes a joke about the joy of being out and about in the sunshine – gallivanting – in the summery day and she, she would give him the care of the children and the bright day and stay in the dark, woody, soap-smelling shop and serve the customers her smile, her wit.

My father squirms and burrows and pushes his hand into his mouth. 'Hungry,' Stuart says, leaning over the pram. 'Hungry wee man?' Everything holds still for midday. The pōhutukawa blooms, the dark and woody shop, the older man, and Stuart and my grandmother, all still. Even John, with his outstretched little hand on a cold bottle of cough syrup. The only movements are the butterfly flickers of my father's eyes. *She'd like sometimes to.* The shadows outside are now directly overhead. Stuart breaks the spell, turns his fine angular face to his sister. 'He's waking,' he says. *Just.* 'Feel free to call in anytime' the old man says, a bit too heartily, and my grandmother prickles, looks around for something small to buy. *To feel free.* But it's good to have him here, Stuart. He, Stuart, helps her navigate the pram through the door. She waves back to him. They smile and Stuart lifts his eyebrows to share a joke (about the old guy). Across oceans, it seems, across all sorts of seas, they wave to each other. Love is funny, my grandmother thinks, there is so much of it. Almost more than you need.

His life was beautiful

> What is the use of the dead talking, if no one has the skill to listen?
> —Hilary Mantel, 'Britain's Last Witch' in *Mantel Pieces*

> Listen, the stream says. *ListenListenListenListen*. I do – or at least, I try to.
> —Doireann Ní Ghríofa, *A Ghost in the Throat*

I heard about Stuart from my grandmother. He was her younger brother, the one with the beautiful, sensitive face, the fourth of the six children. Perhaps he was not quite part of the older group – Jim, Nen and John, who were all strong characters – and not quite one of the lively youngsters – Vida and Douglas. Perhaps he was a kind of middle child, as I am a kind of middle child. The sort of middle child an even-numbered family has. Unlike his father and older brothers who were farmers and hoteliers, Stuart was a chemist. His work was allied to his sisters' work. Like my grandmother, who before she married was a nurse at the Royal Aberdeen Hospital for Sick Children, and like Vida, who drove for the Mechanised Transport Corp during the war, Stuart was a helper. A healer of sorts.

I will start with the end and unfold his life back to its beginning.

On 18 December 1934, Stuart killed himself. He was 30 years old. My grandmother said that it was over a failed love affair. I look on Ancestry.com and find a death certificate. Stuart Johnston (single), Pharmacist (Master), 30 and living with his parents. He died at his work, his chemist shop at 123 Crown Street, Aberdeen. Google Earth shows me a stone corner shop with mullioned windows and two attic room windows peering out from a slate roof.

On that terrible morning, the granite buildings in the street are sharpened by the chill outside; they glint. Christmas lights are strung along the street. He won't notice any of this. It is 8.30, so perhaps before opening time. The woman who, three streets away, is shutting the green door behind her and walking fast through the cold, *perhaps it will snow*, is walking quickly, anxiously towards the chemist, hoping he can give her something to make it go away, like he did last time. A man stands at his second-floor window, smoking. He plans a trip to the chemist to get something for his cold; he wants to be well for Christmas. An old man fingers his coat. He'll go to the chemist to get something for his belly ache. Her sore head, that bruise, that cut, that cramp. Soft cotton wool. Hand cream. She pulls a scrap of paper towards her and makes a list. On the way to get the Christmas tree she'll. He will. They will. Find the door closed. Inside, handsome Stuart has swallowed prussic acid. He would have had it on hand. He is found dead at 1pm, perhaps by his father, who signed the death certificate. Perhaps someone went to get him, Stuart's father, when they couldn't get into the chemist shop. His heavy winter coat bent double. Bent double. His beautiful son.

It wasn't money troubles. He had a decent amount of money for a young man. I know this because I check the £1,615 against the others on the same page of the Scottish National Probate Index. He made his mother executor in March that year and had dated the will again on the day he died. So, he was not broke, and he was thorough. Why was his father not also executor of his will? And who broke his heart so completely that he couldn't live without them. Or did he love men, and so couldn't speak about his love, or the loss of his beloved? Or was it something else? War on the horizon? A family fracture? A perceived failure?

*

When Stuart died my grandmother was in Island Bay, Wellington. It was December so her two boys, John and Jim, were looking forward to staying in Feilding with the couple they are sent to every December who make a nice Christmas for them. In Island Bay the spring winds are dying down and summer is ushering the chill out of the air. My grandmother walks along the Esplanade, her lovely dress blowing against her legs. Perhaps her brother Douglas and my grandfather are walking with her. They walk to the sea, look hard at the waves, find no answer there and walk home again, where there is whisky and gin and tears. And more phone calls. The rent in the universe when someone leaves this way, on the opposite side of the world; it happens both here and there. It is the same tear. Time collapses, and space, and family. What does my seven-year-old father hear? My seven-year-old father with his piano accordion resting against his chest. Sitting on the steps between the house and the garden, the little puffs from the bellows.

I found a notice in the *Aberdeen Press and Journal*, for 7 December 1934, which advertised that Mr Charles A. Michie had sold the business of Chemist and Photographic Dealer to Stuart Johnston. Mr Michie thanked his customers for their patronage and 'hoped that the same generous measure of support may be extended to his successor'. Then Mr Stuart Johnston wrote that he 'hopes by strict attention to the wants of his Customers to merit a fair share of public support'. Further down the page is an advertisement for a Laurel and Hardy film, *Going Bye-Bye*, which is on at the Capitol. A week and a half after they advertise the business changing hands, Stuart takes his life. I imagine he might have been working under Mr Michie, and then Mr Michie retired, and Stuart bought the business off him. What happened? Did buying the business and the heartbreak happen at the same time. Was it that when he needed to pay 'strict attention to the wants of his Customers' he could barely look at his face in the mirror? Did she, or he, come around the night before, when Stuart was looking at his shelves, planning a rearrangement to make the shop really his, to say they didn't, or couldn't, love him anymore? Did he then go home to his parents' house and face his mother and his father whose children were mostly far away, in New Zealand. Did he wonder how he, the currently heartbroken one, could stand in for those missing children. His father's difficult nature, his mother's distant sadness. And his heart so broken. Nobody's fault, not even his, that he couldn't walk into the uncertain, unfolding day splashed with frosty light and yellow snow-clouds and Christmas on the horizon, and live.

In May of 1931, Stuart, who had been living in New Zealand since 1926, arrives back in Scotland. He is 27. He moves in with his parents. He lies in bed with the memory of 40 days of a bunk bed in a cramped cabin vibrating in his tensed body. He tries to relax. It is the first time he's been in their new family home. It is much like the old one, although smaller. There is no room that is his old room. There is a sense that he has gone back to a place, a Scotland, a family, that has, has had to, move on without him. Which is what going back is like. They look at him as though he were run through with their other, faraway children and grandchildren. As though he were hiding them somewhere.

In New Zealand, to begin with, Stuart lived at 39 Derwent Street with my grandparents and their two children. In 1928, his youngest brother, 16-year-old Douglas, arrived at 39 Derwent Street from Scotland and lived with my grandparents. I catch the bus to Island Bay and look at the little white bungalow with its low concrete wall around the front yard. It has maybe three bedrooms and a sleepout, and I wonder how they all fitted in. The house has a corner window with a window seat and a curtain you can pull around it, and I imagine my father sitting there, enjoying the privacy. And I think of my grandmother with her frustrations and longings rippling the surface of things. 39 Derwent Street was first owned by my great-grandfather, and then by my grandfather. It was the original home base for the Johnston family in New Zealand. It helped and housed them until they found their feet. The Scots look after each other in this way. The network holds and houses. But it's not a perfect system. And the damned world won't hold still.

Stuart worked as a chemist in Wellington, possibly the chemist shop at 123 The Parade (he continued living in Island Bay when he shifted out of Derwent Street, so it's possible he worked there, with, oddly, the same street number as his chemist shop in Aberdeen). He had his sister and brother-in-law and nephews and younger brother close by, and an older brother in Dunedin, but then he decided, for some reason, to go home.

While he was in Wellington, Stuart had a whole life, with friends and meals at restaurants, and drinks at pubs. Maybe he played a sport, or belonged to a chess club, or went to hear bands and danced at the local dances. Kissed, and loved, and played up. I imagine he did. And drove north along the Desert Road and noticed the amethyst heather in the foothills. And maybe parked his car and went for a walk into the foothills, the sharp air, the bright, bright light. Maybe took a lover there. Or a good book and found a place on the black thermal earth to lie and read. I imagine this. Because it's not fair to look at a life by its ending. That is not the truth at all. It is the truth then, at that moment, when everything has gone and so you must go yourself. But before then, a whole life happens. He might have encouraged my father with his music. They might have sat at the corner window looking at comics. My father wondering about how his Uncle Stuart mixed potions to make medicines, like a wizard. And my father feeling his loss, just like the rest of them. My grandmother and my grandfather and Douglas, all of whom I knew and also didn't know, gathering at 39 Derwent Street that awful day, and into the evening, where there were tears and silence and there was singing.

In the *Aberdeen Daily Journal*, 15 May 1917, is a piece about a meeting of the Lumphanan School Board who note that four children from Lumphanan School made perfect attendance, and Stuart Johnston is one of them. Beside this piece, there is a long list of British casualties in the War. The list includes officers and rank and file from the Black Watch, the Cameron Highlanders, and the Scots Guards. Some of the casualties in the paper are from the Royal Flying Corps, my grandfather's regiment. Stuart's brother-in-law. You try to keep the world still by things like perfect attendance, studying, a good job, savings, but the damned world won't keep still, and it is bewildering.

Stuart was the last of the Johnston children to be born at the beautiful Mains of Shiels, the large, elegant farmhouse with its granite staircase and fireplaces, and its rich and flowing Aberdeenshire land. A 1901 Scottish Census shows that my great-grandfather, at 28, was head of the family at the Mains of Shiels. They had three servants: Isabella Ewen, William Begg and George Hutcheon. In 1901 my great-grandfather was a farmer, as were his father and grandfather and great-grandfather before him. Into this house and tradition, Stuart is born. In his youth there will be the world wars and the cutting down of men and forests. His landscape will change, utterly. They leave the farm to live above a pub. They are the only hotel in Lumphanan, in the Isla Valley in the Southern

Grampians, where Vida and then Douglas will be born. In a few short years the trees will be cut down to make resources for the war, and to make room for the sheep who come in hordes to trample the places where crops used to grow, where wheat used to shiver and undulate in the winds and breezes. He is, this baby boy, born into the hinge-world, between the Mains of Shiels and the Lumphanan Hotel, between peace and war, between security and difficulty, between Scotland and New Zealand.

At Springbank Cemetery in Aberdeen, my great-grandfather raises a tombstone for Stuart.

Erected by John R. Johnston
In Memory of His Dearly Beloved Son
Stuart Johnston, M.P.S.
Who Died 18th December 1935, Aged 30 Years
His Life Was Beautiful

Suicide was never a crime in Scotland, but in England and Wales it was still a crime when Stuart died, and for nearly three decades afterwards. This criminality is embedded in the language; the word 'committed' fronting the word 'suicide' for decades beyond its decriminalisation. Along with bringing shock and horror and a particularly swerving, unmoored sort of grief, suicide brings guilt – in layers. That you couldn't save them, that you didn't see it coming, that you said or didn't say a particular thing the last time you met. And for some, the archaic shame of someone from their family taking unholy action; as though the very situation is so, so shadowed that it needs some kind of official shadow-container to keep it away from other lives. I applaud my great-grandfather for putting his personal agonies aside to make this strong, loving statement. I applaud the light that he holds to his son's life, telling us, telling me, that his son's life was beautiful. And of that, I have no doubt.

Stuart is the only one of the six children who doesn't have a middle name. I guess, as a Scot, with a name like Stuart, you hardly need an extra one. But it is strange, when the other siblings carry the names of their parents and forebears, that Stuart is just Stuart. Outside of the traditional Scottish naming system. Resident of Scotland and New Zealand. Born into the hinge-time between old and new worlds. A man whose landscape and family and heart were broken.

Six

Sealskin

Wild world

In 2021 I was offered a six-month Creative New Zealand Randell Cottage Writing Residency. This residency saved me in so many ways, not least giving me a lovely Victorian worker's cottage in Wellington to live in while I write this memoir. Tamara and I are sitting in the kitchen of the cottage when Cat Stevens comes on the radio, singing 'Wild World'. We smile. I used to sing this a lot when the kids were young, and I was cooking something or folding something or driving somewhere. I listen to him sing *Now that I've lost everything to you, you say you want to start something new, and it's breaking my heart you're leaving, baby I'm grieving.* We listen on and then, after hearing Cat Stevens sing about it being a wild world, and be careful, and not everyone out there is nice – or words to that effect, I say, 'It's pretty sexist actually.' Tamara looks at me with surprise.

'I mean,' I say, 'he's telling the young woman that it's a dangerous world out there, and he knows about the world and its dangers, and she doesn't. As if a young woman doesn't already know that the world is dangerous.'

Tamara says, 'I always thought it was about a child leaving home.' We look at each other. *History creaks and adjusts.* I quickly feel a little bit guilty that I wasn't always singing about the sadness of children leaving home. *History creaks and adjusts.* It's exhausting imagining you are in charge of the distribution of happiness. *Creaks and adjusts.* That even retrospectively you can damage that happiness. *Creaks and tilts and adjusts. Pause. Adjust.* I think they're right. I think it is about a child leaving home. Is that actually why I was singing it? Through all of those difficult Family Court-ridden years? *History creaks and adjusts.* How impossible to know yourself, let alone anyone else.

*

I am going to be a grandmother. Elliot and Ret tell me by phone from Brisbane. A grandmother. I wish tenderness for my grandchild and its parents. I wish tenderness for us all in this wild world that we keep entering by birth and entering by ship and by plane and entering and re-entering by heart. Perhaps right now everything is all right, with Tamara in the kitchen, and Elliot on the phone, and the next generation, my grandchild, in the making.

The empty Foreign Office

I have been facilitating an online 'poetry appreciation' group since August 2020. We call it the London and Edinburgh Poetry Club and we meet each month to talk about the work of a particular poet. Part of our tradition is to match an alcoholic beverage to the poet. For example, a single malt (and slice of fruit cake) for Ivor Cutler, currant wine for Emily Dickinson, rum for Kei Miller, and a big old cab sav for Seamus Heaney (a single malt might have been closer to the mark, but we needed variety – we had George Mackay Brown and Margaret Tait coming up). There was an in-depth email discussion about the best drink to match Kathleen Jamie's poetry. This from Janet in Edinburgh:

> I found this in an interview from *The Guardian*: 'Jamie often engages Scots speech in her poetry, enjoying the "feel of it and the texture of it in the mouth".' So we need a wine with good complex sensual texture or mouthfeel (yes mouthfeel is one word!) that is like the texture of Scots in your mouth – but Scots has so many textures and nuances –
>
> - definitely not too light, floral or citrus (e.g. not pinot grigio)
> - something big, rich and savoury or spicy in a red – Amarone ? Barbera? (Hugh Johnson recommends a Châteauneuf-du-Pape to go with haggis because of its spiciness and richness)
> - something lively, bright yet flavoursome in a sparkling – Champagne blanc de blanc? (not the Prosecco we get here)
> - something big and sweet in a non-gooey way – really good vintage port? (starts at £50!)

- something flinty to reflect a hard edge to Scots language – Sancerre, Pouilly-Fumé
- a white Rioja? – Marlborough Sauvignon blanc?

Now, from Wellington, at my breakfast time, I join with a cup of Earl Gray tea. Or if I really want to mix it up, a decaf coffee.

Two women in the group work for the Foreign Office in London. One evening, several months into lockdown, one of them told us how when she had gone to her office to pick something up, the Foreign Office building was completely empty, and there was barely anybody on the street. And she said, with some wonder on her face, that the empty Foreign Office building just looked like outdated colonial Britain. And then she repeated that, not in a declarative 'something is over' sort of way, but again in a kind of soft wonder. As though lifting her head above an atmosphere to find another atmosphere. It looked to me like a quiet and complicated Covid-led and Brexit-infused sorrow: for the world, for London, for histories, for all the things we thought immovable – for better or worse – and for this big, empty, suddenly ghostly and haunted building. Then she broke the spell by telling her co-worker that her locker door had been hanging open and there were three pairs of high-heeled shoes inside. We all laughed. And the empty Foreign Office drifted past.

We are both in parts

Lately I have been swimming in Balaena Bay at the bottom of the Roseneath hill in Wellington. There are wooden bathing sheds with slat floors through which you can see the sea washing in and out. Swimming is my therapy. I come out of the sea with my body and my mind washed through and reassembled. After the beach, and in between writing and online teaching, I turn to Vida and keep looking, and if I see her at all (and who knows if I ever do), it's not like I'm orderly, and she is in parts. We are both in parts and making our way towards each other along a small street, zigzagging because there are stones and bricks. There is rubble.

I look through electoral records for Vida's older son Doug, and find an address for him and his wife, along with three other names. I sit looking at the screen and slowly register that I am looking at the names of Vida's grandchildren. I don't know why I didn't find them a year ago. But I didn't. I go to Facebook and quite quickly find Vida's granddaughter, Margaret, who looks a lot like Vida. I send a message and Margaret sends a warm, pleased reply. I say I am writing about Vida; I say I know her life was difficult. I am nervous that she and her two brothers will mind what I am doing, writing about their grandparents. But Margaret says that she will email me with photos and some other information, so I think she is okay with it. After more than a year of searching, I have found a source. I look up from my desk and see the ferry glide behind the Miramar peninsula. If there is no new information, or also if I get a lot of new information, will I lose Vida? Will she slip out of my hands (where she never was) and not come back. Will it be that it wasn't my place to look for her?

I get an email from Margaret. She tells me that her three granddaughters live close by. Close enough to wave to each across the fence during lockdown. She mentions Vida and

Henry's younger child, the one I knew was there but couldn't find. His name is George, and he lives in Canada. I hear that Vida was a character, and that Margaret would have liked to know her better. But after she left her marriage Vida cut herself off from family, except when she was asking for money. I feel a bit sick as I read this part. She says that both Vida and Henry suffered with drink problems. I like how she words this, putting the suffering first.

The part about asking for money makes me think of when I visited my Great-Uncle Jim, my grandmother's brother in Banchory, when I, all of 19 years old and with a crystalline, mostly untried sense of justice, said I wanted to visit Vida. And the look that crossed his face when he said, you don't want to see her. I wonder if the family were worn down by absences followed by requests for money from Vida. Around the questions I already have of when and why Vida left her marriage and whether she saw her children after she left, now circles another question about her grandchildren. I suddenly feel confused, and irritable, and tired.

I drive to the south coast's Ōwhiro Bay, into Te Kopahou Reserve, which is face-on to the gushing, pushing wind off Cook Strait. I take a photo of an oystercatcher hunkered down on a stony ledge that has been pushed up by the sea. I walk into Te Kopahou Reserve's Visitor Centre and two welcome swallows fly in with me and perch on the rafters above my head. They have rosy chests and elegant swallow tails, and they watch me read about the moon and the tidal bulge, and how the tides circle New Zealand. The wind thunders overhead. The welcome swallows watch me leave. It is too windy to walk so I charge back to the car and sit looking out at the stony beach, the thumping waves, the hovering gulls.

What happens to an addict's brain? Does it forget that love, like a mooring rope on a small vessel, connects you to your family, your community? Does it slip that rope, or is it clumsily and by mistake untethered, so it just hangs in the sea beneath the vessel and sometimes in a storm bangs the underside to shock, frighten, and enrage. Does the addict think, why does it bang at me? What has this rope ever done for me? Why do I have to drag it around? And on calm days, does it forget that the rope is hanging there still, because the big quest now isn't love or connection, but the next drink?

I wonder if Vida was kicked out by her husband or if she left voluntarily, perhaps to save her life. Then I remember my own leaving of difficult and angry men and how leaving and being left are often not so black and white, although they can become so in the telling of the story. I wonder if, unlike me, Vida was asking for what she was owed when she asked for money. I start to think about what I have been avoiding thinking about: how Vida lived on the street. What that might mean and how she survived it. I think of doorways and a shared bottle to cut through the cold, and the comfort or economics of another body. Homeless shelters on the harshest nights. There is one thing for sure: Vida was a survivor. You might call her a character. Brash, walking into a room, shoulders back, to make her requests or to set the party going.

Three neat little grandchildren sleeping in their beds on those homeless nights. Where did that live in her? I suppose it lived somewhere, and our hearts should break for her when we think of that place. But I don't know. Don't mothers and grandmothers always, and above everything else, care? Don't we turn naturally, in an animal way, to curl around our young. And then, don't we human animals hang over our young's young to smell them. And lift them. And let the tiny head tip against our neck. And then don't we dip our own head slightly to smell again our young's smell?

*

But that is not the question. It is not even a question.

In Elena Ferrante's novel *The Lost Daughter*, Leda confesses to Nina, a relative stranger (and an exhausted mother), that she is an unnatural mother because she left her daughters and husband to carve out a space for herself in academia. Ferrante dares to suggest that motherhood gives, *and* it takes. I think how mothering is one thing, and one may or may not want to do it, but context is everything, and we know, don't we, that this is still, *still*, a patriarchal and isolating system within which we are asked to be natural mothers.* I am repelled by the thought of leaving two daughters to make a career, but at the same time, I understand it. And once you have broken the family, once you have left the daughters, there's very little chance of going back, not properly, because of external and internal forces – call them judgement, call them righteous anger, call them pain, call them guilt. I do not stand in judgement of Vida for not being part of her grandchildren's lives. The weather, internal and external, most probably did not allow it.

I'm still sitting in the car and the windscreen has a haze of salt spray across it. I am popping Central Otago cherries into my mouth with one hand and spitting the stones into the other hand, the palm of which is stained purple. My phone dings and it's Finola, a poet friend from Glasgow. She's watching a documentary about New Zealand and it's making her think of me. She writes there are black robins and kākāpō. She asks me what I'm doing, and I tell her writing and reading and wondering. Looking out at the stony beach and thinking about Scotland.

*

---

* In an awful resonance, as I am revising this essay, I hear the news that Roe v. Wade has been overturned by the Supreme Court of the United States.

In Edinburgh, after I couldn't get home, and after Vida stepped into the room, I organised a consultation with a friend and wise woman. My friend will not agree that she is psychic, but if she is not, then she is visited by those who can see ahead and behind. I told her about my project, and she started talking about Vida and me, how we have parallel lives, how we are entwined, her in me and me in her. I knew already that Vida's life was more brutal than mine but thought about custody issues and controlling men and bloody breakups, and I could sort of see it. Then I unearthed articles about Vida being up on a drink-driving charge, where she challenges the sheriff in court. Her tone and stance seemed far from mine. Months later, I talk with my friend again and say, *but her life was so dark*. And she was a heavy drinker, and I hardly drink at all. But still, apparently, we are entwined. And now from Margaret I learn that Vida was a 'character', and I know what that can mean. And cutting herself off from family then asking for money seems light years away from anything I might do. The doors to the house of connection and relationship are locked and heavy curtains drawn, and I am outside. I do a couple of laps around the house of connection and relationship and find it ugly. There are other projects. A week passes, and I can't rid myself of the connotations of the word 'character' when it is applied to women. Perhaps characters are women who crash into family silences and turn them into words, who make public the private records, who disrupt a table when they sit at it. The addict usually has a primal wound, and sometimes points to it.

Writing this, I suddenly and strangely have a strong memory of sitting in a wood-and-glass café opposite Melbourne University where I had been tutoring. In front of me is a cup of coffee in a china cup and saucer and a plate with a piece of pistachio biscotti on it. I dip the biscotti in the coffee and bite into the flavours and softened biscuit texture. It's as delicious as I thought it would be. I like the café. I like the jacket I am wearing. I like the orderliness of the place. I like teaching. I like talking about poems and stories. I like containment. Addicts are not contained. Addicts are spillers. Forgetters. Let-downers. They say they will pick you up, or buy the salad, and then they don't. They invite you for dinner and there is no dinner. And you are not allowed to mind. How is my life parallel to Vida's?

Imagine a long silence.

Vida cut herself off from her family. Well, at times I've done the same to some of mine. If a character is someone who speaks her mind and doesn't know when to shut up, I do keep writing my wounds down. I am, I guess, unconventional. I am some sort of homeless, as I currently don't own or rent a home (although this year I have been homeless in Wellington's fanciest suburbs). I think of how Vida left her home, Dunella, which was in one of Aberdeenshire's fanciest suburbs, to live out her life as a peripatetic odd-jobber and homeless person. I have left perfectly presentable middle-class homes to bump around on the margins. Hmm.

After a couple of difficult and angry weeks, weeks where my project turned to sludge and the house of connection and relationship shut me out, I realised something. My only work is to say *yes* to Vida. To her beingness. To her life. And to her suffering. Just as she, by turning up in my flat when I was frightened and alone, with familiar stories and familiar wounds, said *yes* to mine. I am having big and tiring dreams. I read this in Terry Tempest Williams's book *When Women Were Birds*:

> It is the province of mothers to preserve the myth that we are un-burdened with our own problems. Placed in a circle of immunity, we carry only the crises of those

we love. We mask our needs as the needs of others. If ever there was a story without a shadow, it would be this: that we as women exist in direct sunlight only.

Call our shadows sealskins and call us selkies. Call my grandmother's black sealskin coat her shadow. Say, a long time ago, when I was young, she gave it to me, and say I wore it as I walked around in the sharp cold winter light of my country. Say I folded it under my feet as I watched *Macbeth* at Bats Theatre in Wellington. Say I wore it to the train station after the play in a blasting southerly. Say I sat on the train with my mind back there, in the theatre. Say I pulled the little notebook out of the soft pocket of the sealskin coat and started to write.

Turning away

One golden summer day in 2019, I caught the train from Edinburgh to Lockerbie, where a friend picked me up, and we drove across the border into England. We made our way through picturesque countryside and down narrow, tree-lined lanes to reach a country house owned by an elegant barefoot woman wearing a beautiful shawl. We were going to do a soundings session, although I wasn't quite sure what that meant yet and was a bit nervous, worried as I often am about not understanding instructions and getting things wrong. We entered a studio that seemed full of windows and soft light. We moved around the space, our bare feet quiet on the polished wood floors. We joked a bit and laid out the food we had brought for later, then we gathered in a circle. When it came time to make sounds, I followed their lead, but very softly at first and then in gathering confidence. We sang without words, sometimes discordantly, sometimes in surprising harmonies, and sometimes, most wonderfully, in a kind of plainsong. The sun was golden in the room and in the field outside. Towards the end of the session, we lay on the floor and talked about our day in sounds. It seemed both ridiculous and quite a bit closer to the truth than words might have managed. We laughed and commiserated when our host told a story about how she had been shifting heavy stones all morning.

Here, in Wellington, in the kitchen of the Randell Cottage, feeling slightly embarrassed, I start to make sounds. I am surprised at how clear and true they are. I expected them to come out bent and scratchy. I try more sounds and hear my complicated distress make a kind of form, peeling away from my body. I had turned aside from my computer, from Vida.

What if Vida was the boundaryless hard-drinking sort of person that I struggle to be in a room with. The person who, three drinks down, will start to tell you the truth about things, maybe some 'hard facts' they want to pass on, something about life you just don't seem to understand. What then? And so, when I find an article about Vida facing off an official of the court, defending her friend on his drink-driving charge, I stand up from my desk and walk into the kitchen. I make a note – long and clear, and then I break it to go higher. Would I rather she was a teetotal subservient sort, the more traditional, no-trouble-at-all female victim. No, of course I wouldn't. Long, low notes drifting slowly up. I just don't want her to be a drinker, especially of the emphatic sort. Will I still want to tell her story if she is? Is it really her story that I want to tell? Silence. A bee flies through the open door and down the hallway, making its low hum. I have talked about wanting to bring Vida back into family history. I have talked about trying to lift her story to the surface, but I don't know her. Maybe she caused her family endless trouble. I don't know if she was hard and mean, if she was the sort of person who, three sheets to the wind, pins you down and tells you what she thinks. Or worse, what you think. Am I prepared to tell her story (or the little I can see of it) even if it turns out she would, in real life, have made me want to leave the room? I walk down the hall making small breathy notes. Feeling an affinity with Vida has motivated this whole project. I have wanted her to turn towards me. Now I feel myself turn away from her. Why? Because she's not like me? And why would I want her to be like me? I would like her to like me, is what I hear back.

When I read the article about Vida making her slightly inflamed speech in the Sheriff's Office, defending her mate and his careless, alcohol-fuelled event, I felt myself turn away. Now I wonder if it is possible to tell this story without talking about a particular pain that has to do with drinking and amnesia. For that matter, are there ways to talk about Scotland and

New Zealand without talking about drinking and amnesia. If, possibly for reasons of shared ancestry, there's a similar warmth and humour and social ethos between Scots and New Zealanders, there's also a shared tendency, when it comes to pain, to play our cards close to our chest. There is a drinking culture that runs parallel to this tendency. An anaesthetic for the pain of the unsaid. In my childhood home there was drinking, but it came with good food, live music, and warm feelings. No children were harmed in the making. But I also think, as we grew older and joined in, having a drink together was a bit like reciting a creed, it reminded us of what we were raised to believe in. We believed in the primacy of family. The holiness of music. Our place in the circle.

I close the door and stand looking through the stained-glass at the pīwakawaka chasing each other in spirals through the ngaio tree. Five thrushes stab their beaks in Wellington's autumnal, damp grass and boggy soil, and three blackbirds deep in the leaf litter throw leaves impatiently across their shining backs as they look for bugs and worms. They are the true singers. I turn back to my computer, to Vida, hoping that she still allows me access to her. Because what did I expect? A tidy life?

I have a rough night with hardly any sleep and wake up to an email from Grampian Archives saying they've found an entry for Vida: a voluntary admission to Kingseat Mental Hospital in April 1953. I think about dates. I go back to the articles about weddings and divorces and assaults and this admission to Kingseat. I sift through them on the floor. I kneel across the printouts trying to put them in order.

In February 1941, soon after the beginning of the Second World War, Vida divorced Henry on the grounds of cruelty. Cruelty was specific grounds for divorce from 1938 to 1970, and during those years was largely used by women seeking divorce from violent husbands. I imagine that this new category allowed Vida the escape route she hadn't had before. That and the fact that the war gave Vida an income. She started by doing voluntary work as an ambulance driver for Air Raid Precautions (ARP), then, some months before the divorce, she began paid employment working for the Mechanised Transport Corps (MTC). The MTC had its origins in the Women's Legion, and involved women driving ambulances in France, Italy, Kenya, Algeria, Syria, Egypt and Palestine, as well as driving for foreign dignitaries in Britain and various British government departments. Vida was attached to the Norwegian Unit (decamped to Britain after the 1940 invasion of Norway by Germany). This job provided Vida with meaningful, challenging work and her own money. It gave her the chance to leave the violent marriage she had endured for 12 years.

The year following her divorce, there is a picture in the *Aberdeen Evening Express* of Vida shaking hands with the tall and handsome King Haakon of Norway, receiving the King Haakon VII 70th Anniversary Medal awarded in recognition of military personal who served in the Norwegian Armed Forces in Britain, and celebrating the King's 70th birthday.

In January 1946, three months after the end of the war, and six years after their divorce, Vida remarried Henry. I can only imagine that, as for so many women, the end of the war meant the end of work. In my search to discover what happened to MTC drivers after the war, I find a scrap from a newspaper, hard to read, a fragment, a kind of cry, protesting the abrupt dismantling of the MTC. Where to put all that energy, all that camaraderie, all that bravery, all that know-how now? Vida may have had no choice but to go back to Henry. Although I want to argue with her about this. Couldn't she have found a better relationship? But then I think of her sons. It's like they sit down quietly beside me. *We were there*, they say, tipping me towards them. Yes, you were there, I think. In that same year, Henry is convicted of assaulting Vida. I don't know the month of the assault, but I'm guessing that once Vida was under his roof again the violence resumed.

Five years later, there is the article about Vida being convicted of drink-driving. It is titled 'Driver to Norwegian Royal Family During the War; Deeside Woman fined £10' and describes how Vida was seen at nine o'clock at night on Tay Street in Perth 'behaving oddly' and 'talking too loudly'. She got in her car and drove away but was overtaken by police in Scone Street. The article notes that 'for five years [Vida] was official driver to King Haakon and Prince Olav of Norway when they were in the country,' and that in respect of her services to the Norwegian Unit had been awarded a 'pendant medal' which she wore in court. Vida suggested in her defence that the trouble with her driving may have been that 'the steering of the car had a bit more "play" in it than normal'. This suggestion was rejected, and she was fined and banned from driving for a year. In another issue of the same paper, just days later, there was a further piece on this event. It was a correction, made after Vida had written to the paper. It stated that 'As a member of the Mechanised Transport Corps, she was attached to the Norwegian Navy during the war and had the honour, on occasion, to drive Prince Olav. She was not the official driver to the Norwegian Royal family as was stated in Monday's "Evening Express".' I love that Vida wore her medal to her court appearance, and that she had the strength of character to write to the paper – at a time when society might have expected her to be feeling ashamed – to insist that the journalist get their facts right about her war work. The original article about her conviction was given more column inches than its neighbouring article that had the title 'Churchill Top Again: Stalin Out', where Churchill heads the list of 'ten most popular men' in an annual poll taken by the Netherlands Institute of Public Opinion. Stalin had dropped from second place in 1947, to sixth place in 1950, and was now off the top-ten altogether.

In April 1953, the *Evening Express* describes another conviction for assault. Henry pulled Vida out of bed, struck her face with his fists and broke her nose, then dragged her downstairs by her hair. The advocate for Henry said there were faults on both sides, and Henry is released on bail of £5.00. In January of 1955 he brutally assaults Vida again, leading to a conviction and a fine of £12.00. The same advocate says again that there were faults on both sides and goes on to state that, 'Gray should not have used his hands, but it could be said that in view of his wife's conduct, he might on occasion have justification for doing so. Gray found his wife entertaining a man friend and drinking together.' In the same month, Vida entered Kingseat Mental Hospital as a voluntary patient, and left eight days later, 'against medical advice' according to the patient register, saying she was 'relieved' – I guess this means she was relieved to leave. Her stated occupation is 'Home Duties'.

One of the fragments I heard about Vida when I was young was that Henry had her 'admitted' because she was having an affair with a man that she had been a driver for during the war. Perhaps Henry insisted on this 'voluntary' admission, perhaps it was part of her punishment for a real or imagined affair. Or perhaps she admitted herself because she was frightened for her life and didn't have anywhere else to go. Or she may have been mentally ill and needed help. But then, in 1955, the despair caused by 'home duties', domestic violence, coercive control and ever-diminishing possibilities was not usually acknowledged. You could shout into the wind forever – no one would hear you. In many ways, for many women, it is still like that.

It is interesting to notice what does get heard, and how it is heard. In December 1955 there is another article in the *Evening Express*, 'Woman's Verbal Duel With Fiscal' with the subtitle 'Always Teasing, She Says'. The article was not about Thomas Dickson, wayleave officer, the man who was in the Sheriff's Court on a charge of drink-driving, but about Vida, who was a prosecution witness. In Vida's account of the incident, she and a friend, Mrs Leiper, were at Vida's home in the early evening when Thomas Dickson called in. Vida poured them 'two small gins' before going to prepare a meal. Later, the three of them went to the Richmond Arms bar in Culter. As Dickson parked the car outside the bar, he knocked into a public seat, and a policeman came to investigate and then took Dickson to the police station. Two policemen who saw him there formed the opinion that 'he was unfit to be in charge of a car because of drink'. The next day Vida was questioned about the incident at her home by two policemen, one of whom she described as 'very aggressive'. She said that 'they tried to spoon-feed me with my answers, but I wouldn't have any of it. I knew what was the truth and told it to them.' In the trial at the Aberdeen Sheriff Court, there is a suggestion that Vida changed her statement because Dickson phoned her at home when the police where there. She denies that she changed her statement. Vida is 'questioned at length' by the Fiscal, with some focus on her remark to the policeman when he was arresting Dickson that it was 'rather early'. I can't understand what she means by this, and perhaps some of the context for the remark was omitted because it was not suitable for the local paper, but she goes on to say, 'The policeman laughed, I am always teasing.' There is a further confusing interchange about Vida's use of the word 'early' and then at one point she says '"You are rushing me, Mr Fiscal." The fiscal retorts: "Oh no, Mrs Gray, you are rushing me."' It goes on in this strange and unsettling way, and then

Dickson is found not guilty because the judge finds that 'the evidence was largely circumstantial' and 'the Crown has not proved the case'. The article goes on to say that the Sheriff told Dickson: 'You have been mixed up here in a most disgraceful incident, I hope you are thoroughly ashamed of it.' He later says, 'It is, as your agent has said, a borderline case and I am going to give you the benefit of it and I will find you not guilty.' It is a bravura performance of passive language by the judge, which has the effect of distancing Dickson from his crime. It is almost as though Dickson was the good child who the naughty kids – the women who sit in the kitchen to talk, who pour themselves a drink and possibly even have opinions – have lured into misbehaviour. What an old and persistent story it is. When Vida is arrested for drink-driving, she is found guilty (as she probably should have been), fined £10 and loses her license for a year. Dickson gets the benefit of the doubt and is scolded for hanging around with the wrong sort of women. The article, which should have been about Dickson, is about Vida.

I think of Vida, with bruises from her latest beating still on her, entering Kingseat Mental Hospital. There is so much I don't know, but I'm disturbed by my own tendency to feel judgement towards her, like Henry does, like the Fiscal does, like the Sheriff does. To not like her tone. To lose track of Vida's right to be human and to have her own story, in the same way that Thomas Dickson does when he phones Vida when the police are at her home taking her statement. I have my judgemental feelings even though, or perhaps *because*, I recognise that oppressive, mis-shaping, gate-keeping stuff.

There was a day, in the Family Court in Porirua, when I was cross-examined by my ex-partner, Bennett, over the division of custody for our child. To be cross-examined by an ex-partner is no longer allowed in the Family Court, but it was then. I had wondered what to wear that morning even though I'd thought it through carefully the night before. I wore a mint-green cardigan, buttoned up, and a skirt. The cardigan was wrong, I realised, too late. Not sombre enough, and possibly too feminine. As I sat there in the court, the mint-green cardigan started to feel like something that Marilyn Monroe might have worn in *Some Like It Hot*. Bennett, who didn't pay child support and didn't offer any other help financially, cross-examined me, focusing on why I had shifted house so many times, the subtext being the effect that might have on our child. I was renting, and he owned his own home. I was trying to raise two kids on a benefit, and he was working fulltime as a psychologist, sometimes as an expert witness in the Family Court. The judge, an old man, his head floating above the long shining bench, listened to it all, the talk and the silences. Bennett on one side of the bench, me on the other. Me unable to answer why I had shifted so many times. Completely unable to find the words. But lately I have been hanging out with Vida, and she is crazy-wonderful brave. When she's in the mood, she has been giving me lessons. I make a long, sweet note, broken at the end. There are 12 tūī with their double voice boxes in the ngaio tree. There are 24 voice boxes vibrating in the ngaio tree. Of course I couldn't find the words. How could I speak about my difficult circumstances to the man who was helping to create them. How would he hear me? Where would my words land? Ask me now.

Tremble tremble, the witches have returned!

> Something in us dies with Macbeth: call it ambition or the iniquity of an imagination that does not know how to stop.
> —Harold Bloom, *Macbeth: A Dagger of the Mind*

I'm sick of sitting at this desk. Really, I'm sick of writing about violence against women. I walk around the room, then crouch down to stretch my lower back, and crouching shakes free a memory: *A giant woman crouches across from me and opens her mouth.*

In 2017 I saw an art installation at the Talbot Rice Gallery in Old College, University of Edinburgh called *Tremble Tremble*, by Irish artist Jesse Jones. Made during a heated abortion debate in Ireland, it explored the historical oppression of women. You entered the exhibition space by pushing aside a black curtain. On opposing floor-to-ceiling screens was a towering, muscular, marvellous witch. A giant of a woman. Not static, but moving. Not silent, but speaking. As she crouched and stood and leaned towards us, she quoted from the 1487 *Malleus Maleficarum*, the guide to identifying, accusing and executing 'witches'. But as she quotes from *Malleus Maleficarum*, she mixes up its words. The witch. The disruptor. In the central space were circular curtains with an image of two massive arms on them, and as you stepped towards the curtains, performers opened and then closed them around you, and you stood, encircled, hained, while plumes of smoke rose from a crack in the floor, the crack representing the chasm over which sat the Oracle of Delphi, articulating the prophecies that rose from it.

And a female seer enters the Old College.

Feeling a fish-flicker of fear from the containment, I stood inside the curtains, straddling the smoke.

Artefacts were set out around the gallery like runes, including, specifically for the Scottish installation, a scold's bridle, an iron instrument of torture used to silence and humiliate outspoken, disobedient women. On screen, the witch walked among the rubble of a courthouse. She raised a leg and stomped down hard. There was a soundtrack to the exhibition in the form of testimony spoken in courtrooms by women accused of witchcraft. This by Temperance Lloyd, a woman hanged for a witch in 1682:

> *Did I disturb ye good people? I hopes I disturb ye, I hopes I disturb ye enough to want to see this, your house, in ruins all around ye! Have you had enough yet? Or do you still have time for chaos?*

The exhibition bites deep into the theatre of the witch hunts and meets theatre with theatre. I thought about the fear in those who make and hold on to structures of power: church, court, the patriarchy. What are those things but brute buildings if they disallow the feminine? You cannot compartmentalise, contain, own, or re-make the divine. The divine drifts in like incense and lifts the hair of the gatekeepers. When the feminine divine is denied, it acts like a memory, it appears like a prophecy.

Tremble Tremble takes its title from the Italian 1970s 'Wages for Housework' campaign, where the campaigning women chanted 'Tremate tremate, le streghe sono tornate!' (Tremble, tremble, the witches have returned!). Returned even to the heart of the light, the bright, the burning, to Old College, Edinburgh University, just a five-minute walk from Edinburgh Castle's ashy forecourt. Sylvia Federici is the writer, teacher and activist who led the 'Wages for Housework' campaign. In her book *Witches, Witch-Hunting, and Women*, I read about the land enclosures, the loss of the commons. Federici claims that the enclosures marked the beginning of capitalism, a revolution that needed a constant workforce who would be fed and clothed by unpaid domestic workers. It is not news that the Western history of witch hunts springs from issues of land and ownership. But for me, it made sudden sense to discover that the land enclosures in Britain marked the beginning of a new institutional violence against women.

In the late 15th century landlords and well-off peasants began fencing off undivided common land to put into individual ownership. The land included previously shared fields, heaths, moors, fens and wasteland. In the fencing off of common land, communal obligations, privileges and rights were lost. Farmers and peasants were pushed off the land they depended on for their survival. Older women who had hitherto been cared for in the communal system were plunged into poverty and homelessness. But these old women, unused to such treatment, made their displeasure felt (a raised voice, a foot-stomp), and thus older women were the first to have the shaky finger of righteousness pointed at them, to be marked out as witches and tortured and murdered as such. Any power that didn't fall under the boundary of state and church was, Federici writes, 'suspect of diabolism'. Women who didn't join the 'war against witches' and accept the leadership of men were in danger because 'once it was accepted that women could become servants of the Devil, suspicion of diabolism would accompany a woman every moment of her life'.

Seeing *Tremble Tremble* and reading Federici's book helped me to understand deep in my bones how the witch can be both a symbol for the hatred and oppression of women – the witch-hunts – and a disrupter of those oppressions. I make myself a timeline to see how things unfolded during and after the enclosures in 16th- and early 17th-century Scotland:

1560 The puritanical Scottish Reformation Parliament established the Scottish Presbyterian Kirk, creating restrictive laws around the arts, education, architecture and 'morality'.

1563 The Scottish Witchcraft Act made practising witchcraft and consulting with witches a capital offense.

1590 The North Berwick witch trials were held, instigated by King James VI.

1597 Scotland's King James VI's tract against witches, *Daemonologie*, was published.

Last night I was reading Rachel Cusk's novel *Second Place*, and on page 152 I stopped and laid the book down on my lap.

I had read the part, only addressed in one paragraph, about the narrator's ex-husband not returning their four-year-old daughter at the agreed time. He had their daughter phone her mother to tell her that she didn't need to be picked up, and he went on to keep the child for a year. I thought how this is a contemporary version of torturing the witch – if the witch is defined as a woman outside of the control of a man. I thought of the shock when Tamara was not returned on time, and changes were made without negotiation, and how that moment marked the beginning of ever more complex living arrangements for our child. Like the woman in Cusk's novel, I too had a phone call from my child from their father's place, when they were around seven years old, to tell me the results of a Family Court division of custody decision that didn't go my way, or, to my mind, Tamara's way. I can still hear the discomfort in their voice as they delivered the information, passed on to them by their father, information they understood barely at all and yet understood all too well. I pick rosemary for remembrance for all of the tortured mothers and children and put it in a vase. I light a beeswax candle. I crouch in my room in Wellington and the giant also crouches. She leans towards me and I towards her. She lifts her great arms and holds my shoulders with the flat of her palms; she props me up. This speaking, spreading witch shows me that she is big enough to carry not only my fury, but Vida's, and not only our furies, but the terrors that have spiralled through our DNA from the burning days. I lean into her big, encircling, strong arms.

Apology

On 25 May 2022 the Church of Scotland acknowledged and expressed regret for the terrible wrongs done to women accused of witchcraft and the church's role in this historical persecution. The motion was brought forward by Reverend Professor Susan Hardman and was accepted by the General Assembly of the Church of Scotland.

A candle is lit in the Church of Scotland.

Seven

An ache for the land

Heather

> This New Road will some day be the Old Road, too
> —Neil Munro, *The New Road*

The cicadas are roaring, the sun is rising, and already, before eight in the morning, I feel its sharp heat on my arm and the side of my face. I put my sunglasses on, adjust the sun visor, and know it's going to be a long drive. But I'm heading north, and in a few hours the monotony of field after field, cow after cow, macrocarpa windbreak after macrocarpa windbreak, will be broken by the sharp white-and-blue summit of Mt Ruapehu breaching the green hills. And soon after, when I'm on the Desert Road driving through the Central Volcanic Plateau, I will see the heather, the ling.

The heather on the Central Plateau is the same 'ling' that Aberdeen-born Nan Shepherd writes of in her wonderful book about the Cairngorm mountains, *The Living Mountain*. Shepherd writes of the amethyst ling, and its 'heady' perfume, and how as she walks through the ling 'one walks surrounded by one's own aura of heather scent'. Shepherd tempers a capacity for ecstasy with a sharp, scientific eye, and keeps both in balance with a very Scottish sensibility. After describing the joys of walking barefoot through the heather's perfumed cloud of pollen, she warns that too much of it can 'stupefy' the body. 'Like too much incense in church,' she writes 'it blunts the sharp edge of adoration, which, at its finest, demands clarity of the intellect as well as the surge of emotion.'

Shepherd spent years walking in the Cairngorms, a mountain range between the Spey and Dee river valleys in the Highlands of Scotland, and, across years of looking and listening and noticing, she came to understand that the mountains were a complete and interwoven ecosystem: an ecosystem, if we would just imagine it, that could also include us. But as she was writing the Second World War was playing out. In the countryside surrounding her home, as in other parts of Scotland, trees were being felled, as they had been during the previous World War, changing the landscape and the soil composition and devastating small farms in Aberdeenshire. Through that time of disorder, Shepherd continued to pay close attention to nature, noticing the changes as the living mountain lived. The power of this quiet act of attention resonates today and will do so, I expect, far into the future.

Around the time Shepherd was walking through heather in the Cairngorms, seeds from the same plant were being dispersed by wind across the Central Volcanic Plateau in New Zealand. Heather was introduced there in the early 20th century by an Edinburgh man hoping to recreate Scottish grouse moors in New Zealand. The grouse didn't naturalise, but the heather did. 'Scotch heather' is now considered a biosecurity risk in New Zealand. Growing together in stands, it shades out native plants like hebes, inhibiting their growth.

Recent scientific research describes invasive weeds like heather disrupting communication between natives. It does this by depleting them of nutrients which makes them 'go quiet'. Plants use volatiles or scents emitted through leaves and roots to call for help when they are being attacked by insects, to attract pollinators, and generally to communicate on the overground and underground web. When plants go quiet, they reduce their emission of volatiles. They are less able to 'call' to each other, and most importantly less able to call to their specific kin, to parents and siblings who would normally share nutrients with them. Attempts to introduce bio control in the form of insects that naturally control the growth of heather in the UK failed because the introduced plants were 'calling' differently. In adjusting to a very different environment, they had changed chemically, so they no longer acted or smelled the same. Heather in the sharp, bright, unfiltered light of Aotearoa New Zealand's Central Plateau sings a very different song than its ancestor did in the muted moody Scottish Highlands. So heather still drifts across that stretch of high tussock land with its black pumice-pitted soil and sulphurous breakthroughs of thermal steam that stain the fissured land with a violent yellow. Heather grows in that simmering landscape – some of the most active land in the world – touching Mt Tongariro, Mt Ngāuruhoe, and Mt Ruapehu to one side, and the Kaimanawa Mountains to the other.

Just before the Desert Road I stop at the National Army Museum, Te Mata Toa, for a pee. I don't go through the exhibits, I don't feel like looking at soldiers and rations and wounds today, although I have at other times, with the kids when they were little. Never particularly voluntarily. I try not to think too hard about the Central Plateau being a military training area. But then, outside of the bunker-style museum, beside a famous cannon, I run my hand through a rose-gold tussock and feel a stab of love, a kind of euphoric love for this piece of volcanic country, for its blue-and-white mountains and black-and-gold plains, for its museum the colour of the volcanic soil it rests on, for its wild Kaimanawa horses, and for the heather I once enjoyed, before I knew better. The love comes suddenly, a hit on the lungs. I take a photo of tussock, of mountains, of close and far. As if I could hold it still, explain it and share it. As if I could hold out my country, my Aotearoa New Zealand, and say, *look*, this is my place. I scrabble for some of Shepherd's clarity of intellect to temper the surge of emotion.

In *The White Bird Passes*, Jessie Kesson, herself a friend of Nan Shepherd, describes a childhood spent in the shadow of the Cairngorm Mountains in an orphanage in Skene, Aberdeenshire. For Janie, the Cairngorms are a dark wall blocking out the rest of the world. Despite their looming presence, she never gets close enough to see them open out, to gain feature and nuance. She is not close enough to explore their foothills, to see their lochs and corries, or to walk through the heather. The heather in this novel is hidden behind distance and mist. What the novel does reveal is how the land can carry pain, both with us and for us.

The land carried Janie's pain: the pain of being taken from her mother and put into the orphanage, and the pain for her mother, left on her own. On her last day at the orphanage, Janie notices that the Cairngorms were closing in and 'pressing down on the howe'. She writes that 'Silence had circled all the land, and held it, trembling prisoner'. And in the stubble of a field a peesie cried, revealing 'Some long, long grief that had found an echo in Janie herself. Her pain became submerged in the peesie's cry. Herself and the landscape had stood in some ache, waiting for release.' The ache of being held prisoner in silence and loss is a shared grief between Janie and the land. And as they grieve the loss of personal kin, of vital community, each becomes the other, each carries the other.

An ache for and of the land is at the heart of Lewis Grassic Gibbon's *Sunset Song*, which is both a praise poem to Kincardineshire's land and people and songs – a particular and precious ecosystem – and a lament for the damage done to that ecosystem in the First World War. The stretches of corn that rippled like water across the land could no longer grow after forests were felled and sheep were brought in. The local minister – a new, impassioned minister – laments the loss of landscape and lifestyle. In his first sermon he cries out that, '*They have made a desert and they call it peace*; and some had no liking of the creature for that, but God! there was truth in his speak.' The character Chae, a tenant farmer with socialist principles who knew the folksongs, comes home on leave to a farm shorn of its woods. He looks around and laments the destruction and the greed, and that 'the whole bit place would soon be a waste with the wind a-blow over heath and heather where once the corn came green'.

These books show me how to manage both my closeness to the land and my distance from it, how my imagination springs from the land and returns to it. The closeness and the distance equally full of wonder and of pain. And these stories of an aching land evoke the ache of this land, of Aotearoa, where so many forests and their deeply entangled, communicating, caretaking networks were cleared by settlers to make way for paddocks and sheep.

Soon after my family landed in New Zealand from Aberdeenshire, in 1926, they took a trip to Rotorua, a city within the Central Plateau. I have a photo of them standing outside the wharenui of a marae at Whakarewarewa village. The men are dressed in suits and trilbies, my great-grandmother, my grandmother and Vida in fashionable 20s dresses and cloche hats and coats with fur-trimmed collars. Around them, outside the photo, is the thermal land, its earthy smells, vivid colours and drifting steam, its crystalline pools and boiling mud. They would have travelled to Rotorua by car or train, and they might have seen the heather that was settling into the land on the Desert Road, a pop of amethyst through the tussock, and I wonder how that sight landed in them – with a bump of pain for what they'd left behind, or a small shock of pleasure for what could be carried over to this new land. Might they have laughed at it and made a joke along the lines of 'How far does a person have to travel to get away from that stuff!' But actually, it wasn't even that cohesive. Not everybody's minds would have been on settlement and homesickness, because the family was already forming its division, those who were going to stay and those who were going home.

In the photograph, my great-grandfather is looking off to the side, not at the camera, and he looks burdened. He had come out to New Zealand months before the rest of his family to buy a farm in the South Island. His family had followed. It hadn't worked out – the Depression was reaching New Zealand, and also a farm in the South Island of New Zealand is such a different prospect to a farm in Aberdeenshire where he was used to farming. So, already he would have been planning the return trip to Scotland. And already my grandparents would have said they were going to stay on in New Zealand. Vida, too young to decide for herself, was going back and would have been looking at her sister, Nen, and preparing herself for goodbyes. Home meant two different places now. Of course, I don't know if Vida was relieved to return home. Perhaps Scotland seemed a better option to her after a few strange months in the country that was going to be home and now was not. If there was a freshness and freedom in New Zealand, it might also have felt empty and uninscribed compared to Scotland: the houses on the hills and the buildings at the port like writing in water, almost on the point of disappearing even as they were made. She was only in New Zealand for four months, but a lot can be felt about a place in a short time. New Zealand might have worked out better for her. But then, a connection to place has little to do with practicalities; place inhabits us in particular ways. Sometimes you need to walk across the dimmed midwinter heather on the moorland you have always known, you need to feel it there because it made you, because you remember breathing with it, and because of the way it pressed you upwards towards the great expanse of the sky. The land reminds us of people and times and landscapes that have gone. That is why some of us can't leave, and others of us can't stay.

*

For at least a decade, Vida and Nan Shepherd lived within kilometres of each other in neighbouring Aberdeen suburbs. Nan Shepherd lecturing in English at the Aberdeen College of Education, and going to her beloved Cairngorms to walk and to notice and then to write. A few kilometres away in Dunella, Vida was on 'domestic duties,' having children, taking beatings and refusing to lie down, refusing to be quiet. There are a thousand ways to be invaded. There are a thousand ways to lose communication with your kin. I would love to know if Vida ever drove herself to the Cairngorms; if she liked to walk through heather. I think that she might laugh at me for that.

Years ago, on the way home from a cheap single-parent-style winter holiday in the Central Plateau, I pulled into a layby on the Desert Road and watched my kids take their pillows from the car and walk over some small black-soil rises, then lie down with their pillows on the frosty tussock, as if to sleep there. The sulphur smell at their nostrils, the cold circling sky above; moored and released by the land.

One wee queenie

Vida's granddaughter Margaret has sent me a copy of Vida's table plan for a 'Birthday Party at Dumbuck Hotel, Dumbarton, Thursday 6th April, 1944'. It is a 15th-birthday party for Doug, her eldest son. The plan is typed up; the title and date underlined by repeated dashes. The table is carefully outlined with ruled lines, and typed names drop down each side of it. All of the names on the party plan fit nicely on the page, none of them bumping into the lines of the table, or sitting hard against the far margin. There are 20 at table. At one end is Doug, and at the other is Vida. Aside from Doug's younger brother, George, most of the guests are from the Free Norwegian Navy that Vida is attached to as a driver in the Mechanised Transport Corps. Guests include Sub. Lieut. Haalstad and Mrs Haalstad, Mrs Robertstad, Lieut. Strøm, Lieut. Gidske, and Commander Knudtzen. The other names are more Scottish: Mrs Macphie, and her husband Provost Macphie, for example. As I look at the page I see Doug, at the head of the table, glance at George, who is second on his left down the table between Mrs. Buchanan and Lieut. Strøm. Perhaps both are wondering when they can go home to their father and the housekeeper at Dunella and ride their bikes. Vida at the other end, is well dressed, playful, proud.

    I think Vida had a talent for raising spirits in hard times. Actually, I don't just think this, I know it because copies from Vida's autograph book (another newly acquired treasure from Margaret) tell me so. Here is one message from the Captain of the Norwegian warship, Spinanger:

> Mrs Vida Gray!
> Come to Norway one day, when I am home, so I can repay some of the great pleasure and happiness you

have given to the Norwegians, during the five years of occupation of our lovely country. Sept. 29th 1945.

Jørgen Eikanger
Spinanger – Bergen

In January 1945, Margaret Macleod writes:

> Never did so many owe to one 'Wee Queenie' so much as all owe to 'Vida'

I don't know who Margaret Macleod is, perhaps another MTC driver. I do know that in the Aberdeenshire Doric dialect, girls and young women are referred to as quines, which is, I think, what 'Queenie' refers to here, referencing Vida's Aberdeenshire roots. And I don't think it is merely party-girl bonhomie that they're responding to in these messages. I think she was a generous soul.

If I wish that Vida had invited a few of Doug's friends to the party, well, perhaps she just couldn't. Perhaps she was living in Glasgow for her job and too far away from her son's friends back in Aberdeenshire. Or she was just too fractured or too exiled from that old life to be contacting her son's friends and their parents. But she did put some thought into the arrangement of this party, and it would, I'm fairly certain of this, have been fun, for the adults at least. The boys may have felt out of place. Vida may have been trying to fit square pegs into round holes, old lives into new lives, to firm up dissolving shapes. I remember this myself, how some of my children's birthdays post-separation were clumsily divided between parents, or missing a parent, or missing friends. We do what we can do. I salute Vida for deciding to at least introduce her two sons – who were becoming young men in the shadow of the war – to her new friends who had found shelter in Scotland while their country was occupied, and who came to the table bringing the whiff of different, more faraway worlds. I think these men would have been kind to the boys. Even the wrong-shaped gathering can bring new perspectives.

Dumbuck Hotel where they held Doug's party is in Dumbarton, a town on the north bank of the River Clyde, near Glasgow. On the first page of Vida's autograph book, under the heading 'Souvenirs of my Services as M.T.C. Driver', is a picture of the Norwegian Navy Gunnery lined up outside an imposing brick building called Helensee House. Helensee House, once a mansion house and then a school for boys, became in the Second World War a base for a detachment from the Free Norwegian Army.

Next to the picture of Helensee House is the signature of King Haakon of Norway. On another page headed 'Halcyon days and memories sweet, July 1945' is a picture of Vida's two tall and slender sons standing between a Captain Hansen, and another man, 'Arthur' – whose name is mostly rubbed out. Apparently Vida wanted to marry one of the men she drove for during the war, but they couldn't marry because she was divorced and the man was Catholic. I go through the photos Margaret has sent me, and put four of them side by side: the one with Captain Hansen and Arthur, two with Arthur, Vida and her boys on Ben Lomond, and one with Vida, the boys and Arthur all relaxing in deck chairs. I think I have found the man who Vida loved and wanted to marry. Arthur is intelligent-looking and – although this is hard to define and easy to get wrong – he looks kind. She looks undefended, but in a good way. She looks to be herself.

In the photos at the top of Ben Lomond, Vida is wearing casual trousers, a loosely tucked shirt and a cap. This is the moment when her life might have changed. She might have married Arthur and been happy, and safe. She might have ended up living in Norway, or he might have stayed in Scotland. She might have married a man who knew her as a woman with a job that required bravery and skill, and a woman who could draw people together in the best way. A very different context to the girl who, on her 19th birthday, got married to get out of travelling to New Zealand again with her family. Because this is another piece of new information: Vida's parents would only let her stay in Scotland while they went travelling if she was married. I look again at the photo of Vida in her elegant 1920s wedding gown, her graceful long-limbed pose on a low stool, Henry standing behind her. So the marriage on her 19th birthday was more a bid for freedom than anything else. A desire to stay put, to escape her parents, and to live a little. Her body so easily arranged for the photos. That night, she unpinned the lover's knot of orange blossom that held her veil in place and stepped out of her wedding dress into her new life, and in the morning, 17 years later, pulled on her button-up trousers, a loose shirt and a cap, put on some lipstick, and drove to Glasgow Queen Street railway station to pick up her sons. Then she picked up Arthur, and the four of them drove to the foot of Ben Lomond. They piled out of the car into a summer day in the Highlands and set out to climb the most southerly of the 'Munros', stepping through the purple ling as they did so, releasing its intoxicating fragrance.

In the photograph Vida's walking clothes are well worn. Vida liked to walk. So perhaps when she lived at Dunella she *did* walk in the Cairngorms enjoying the heady scent of the heather, while at a colder elevation Nan Shepherd stood at the edge of a crystal-clear linn on a mountainside, translating the language of water. Vida wanted to stay in Scotland and unfold her life into its cities, its cars and wars and houses and bunkers and fields and mountains. She wanted to stay in Scotland for her loves and losses, failures and wins. She chose Scotland and marriage over the long voyage to New Zealand, where her sister and two nephews, one of them my father, were living their different lives.

On the property of Helensee House there was a fernery, which is described by Donald MacLeod in his publication *Dumbarton, Ancient and Modern* (1893) as 'possibly the finest collection of New Zealand ferns in Great Britain'. The fernery was 51 feet long by 30 feet wide and was sunk below the level of the surrounding ground. I don't know if it was still there when the Norwegian Navy was in residence, but I imagine it was destroyed by the first or second world wars, or was just abandoned because the colonial fervour for collecting specimens from other countries had died down. I think of ponga – there would have been ponga – their seeds tucked into the earth that, without the temperate world the greenhouse offered, stay tucked and enfolded. And in the cold earth, in that place where boys learned to be boys and men to be men, the seeds of the silver ferns have a memory of mists, of green, of dappled light, of movement, of lift and fall, of breathing.

Ōtepoti/Dunedin

> Our folk are on the old drove road – the ghosts of them,
> the hunters and the tribes long-perished to the eye
> —Neil Munro, *The New Road*

I take a trip to Ōtepoti Dunedin to meet my grandmother and Vida's nephew, Jack, and his daughter Karen. When Karen answers the door of her father's house, I see my grandmother's face. And when I meet Jack, there is her face again. The heart-shaped, high cheek-boned Johnston face. Karen brings out tea and cream buns, and we begin to get to know each other. I tell Jack that I don't remember meeting him in the past, and he says that they didn't keep up much with the North Island family.

Jack's father, John, was the very first of my family to come to New Zealand from Scotland. He was 22, and New Zealand was his second migration attempt; he'd already tried living in Canada, but Dunedin, New Zealand became home. Although not without one more migration back to Scotland. In May 1934, with high unemployment in New Zealand, John travelled back to the UK with his wife Hellen and his son Jack – the Jack I was eating cream buns with. John began running a pub in Turriff, Aberdeenshire. Jack tells me that he doesn't remember much of this time in Scotland except how, when he was about four years old, he would dance along the length of the pub counter to entertain the patrons and was paid a penny for his efforts. This makes me think of Bill Manhire's essay 'Under the Influence' where he describes being 'hauled out of bed' by his publican father 'late at night and led through to the bar to sing the "Invercargill March"'. We Davidson kids also did our fair share of late-night performances, although in a family living room not the family pub.

They were five years in Turriff, perhaps thinking that

Scotland was, after all, the better bet. But then war arrived, again. On 8 November 1939, two months after the beginning of the Second World War, John, his wife Hellen and their three children Jack, seven, Vida, four, and Stuart, an infant, leave Scotland for New Zealand. The four-year-old girl is named for her Aunt Vida (my Vida), who at this point is driving ambulances for Air Raid Precautions, the baby for his Uncle Stuart who is three years dead, and John (Jack) for his father and grandfather. Jack, buttoned into his warm coat, stands at the railings of the *Rangitane* holding his father's hand as they leave the docks of London; too old now, at seven, to dance across pub counters. Jack, who is looking a little tired, tells me that the Germans sunk the Rangitane on the return journey. Later, I find an article saying that the Rangitane was sunk by Germans on November 24, 1940, 300 miles east of New Zealand. Oh, little family, transporting precious names across perilous oceans on the warm, animal bodies of children.

I take the bus to Morningside, recognising all of the Edinburgh names in this 'Edinburgh of the South' which has lately reclaimed its original name, Ōtepoti. It is a city with a strong and independent personality. So, the Edinburgh names are not quite ghosts of the old country, that would be to insult the city, and yet in some ways they *are* a harkening to old forms, old insistences, underneath which other names push and rise like trees growing through and around old roads.

The bus stops, and I step off it and as both feet hit the pavement, I find that I am standing directly in front of 31 Elgin Road, the house I had set out to find. The gate is a lovely marine blue and has on it, in brass, the number 31. The house is a double-gabled wooden villa, trimmed in the same marine blue. On either side of the gate and along the stretch of road for the entire block is a thick, tall holly hedge. Much taller than me. This is the house that Jack's father bought. It is where Jack and his siblings grew up. Did my father visit this place? Did he hang out with his cousins here? I feel like I am standing outside a castle surrounded by brambles. This is partly to do with the fairy tale way that the glossy holly hedge and the bright blue gate manifested in front of me when I got off the bus. I think, someone should notice me, recognise me, and invite me in.

I have been reading *The New Road* by Neil Munro, about General Wade's 'new road' built through the Highlands in Jacobite Scotland. Bands (or Watches) of Highlanders unmaking the road as it was built or making use of the new road to smuggle and trade. Eventually, though, the roads and bridges through the mountains were significant in the destruction of the clan system, as was planned. In the novel, if you are travelling in the Highlands and are a fellow clansperson or connected because you are somebody's uncle or niece, or somebody is your father or grandmother or great-grandfather, you are given entry to homes and to hospitality. Even in the barest places. Whether they trust you or not. I press the tip of one finger on a dark-green scalloped holly leaf. I feel that somebody should call me in. The great hedge delineates a definite outside, where I am standing, and an inside where some kid is watching cartoons on a wide screen TV. I have a strange feeling that if I were bold enough to just push open the gate of 31 Elgin Road, I would be in Scotland again. It makes no sense, but I have a strong feeling, not of home, but of proximity to home, to a land beloved and familiar; as though I would break into wholeness something that had been divided: Scotland and New Zealand, the North and the South.

Gaelic psalm singing

It is another bright, warm, uncharacteristically still Wellington night, and a ferry glides out of the dark harbour on a line of its own light. I have been reading *Grand Hills for Sheep*, written by Georgina McDonald and published by Whitcombe and Tombs in 1949. It has a beautiful Russell Clark woodcut cover with three sober faces looking out into the Otago hills. It is about Scottish settlers, three brothers, two wives, a daughter, who in 1848 sailed to New Zealand and settled in Central Otago. In chapter five, the small community of folk go to their little church in thick driving rain. I read that in the church

> The precentor took his place for the final psalm; the congregation rose to pray and for the parting blessing; then, with a seemly pause of reluctance to leave the House of God, they paced slowly out into the rain.

In the ancient practice of Gaelic psalm singing, the precentor stands at the front of the church and sings two lines (in a melody he decides on in the moment), and then the congregation, a cappella, respond to the lines with their own variations. I have heard, via YouTube, Scottish Gaelic psalm singing in a Free Church on the Isle of Lewis. The 'called' lines are simple, crying things that are lifted by the congregation who worship with them, embellishing the lines with layered harmonics. It creates a haunting, haunted, spiritual music which conjures up the cold, shapely, bird-rich Hebridean islands from whence it comes. I didn't know that this sound had also called across Central Otago, the old psalms meeting this unknown land and beginning to make its shape, like a fall of snow.

Forgieside

I have a Zoom conversation with my brother, Ron, and his wife, Trish. They are at their home in Waipū, Northland, on a piece of land they call Forgieside after our Davidson great-grandparents' farm in Keith, in the Northeastern Highlands. Their house sits at the top of a small hill with a sweep of kawa poplars on one side and the sea on the other. The house, practically all windows, feels like a bridge to both views, the leafy and the wavey.

I want to ask Ron if he knows how Uncle John, Dad's brother, died. I know it was a car accident in 1977 when he was 52, but something nags at me about it. Something withheld or a fragment overheard. I was told he had a heart attack while driving. No, Ron shakes his head. He'd been drinking with his mother, our grandmother, and when he drove away that day, at a turn on a road not far from her house, he had the car crash that ended his life. I feel a thump of horror and a rush of pity at the same time. After John's death, when Mum and Dad visited my grandmother, they heard her crying herself to sleep at night. Another enfolded piece of family history.

If there was a place to send a letter, I think my grandmother would have written to her sister, Vida, to tell her what had happened. When she could bear to write the letter and send it. And Vida would have wept for the infant she had helped to entertain on that long voyage from Scotland to New Zealand in 1926. Perhaps Vida wrote back. What did they say to each other?

Islands

> From the mainland it glows with an inner light, like a piece of uncut amethyst laid on the sea
> —Marion Campbell, 'Islay of the Kings' *Argyll: The Enduring Heartland*

Eldon is half-brother to my son Elliot and 16 years his junior. He is visiting New Zealand from his home in Shetland, and he's doing it the hard way, during Covid. I meet him in Wellington before he heads back to Scotland to begin his Business Studies degree at Glasgow's University of Strathclyde. We've met before, but years ago, and now he's a young adult. He parks his bike, comes into the café, scans in, turns around, and turns into his father. Same face, colouring, and gestures as Kester, but in the lanky phase, before bulking up into a man. The small, initial awkwardness clears, and we start chatting. Eldon has been staying with his father's family in Christchurch. He tells me how one of his aunt's children was wearing a cap with a British Petroleum sunburst logo on it that Eldon realised would have come from his dad, from when Kester worked in the oil and gas industry in Shetland. Lots of kids at Eldon's school wore caps and sweatshirts with the BP logo on them.

Eldon arrived in New Zealand just weeks before I got back to New Zealand from Edinburgh, so we share managed isolation stories. Eldon laughs about having his temperature taken by a soldier who aimed the thermometer at his head as though it were a gun. I share my story of the tired nurse who held her blue sharpie up to my forehead instead of the thermometer. His plan is to travel home via Brisbane, where he'll spend time with Elliot and Ret. But every and all things are chancy these days. He could maybe not get to Brisbane as Covid cases in the community means that currently the travel bubble between

New Zealand and Queensland is suspended. Or the UK may re-classify Brisbane from green to amber in which case he'll have to self-isolate when he gets home, unless there are community cases in which case he'll have to go into managed isolation (and may or may not have to pay for it depending on where in his travels he is when the change happens). If Brisbane should become red-listed while he is there, he won't get out anyway until the classification changes.

This head-spinning complexity makes me think about when Kester died and Elliot, at 26, flew from New Zealand to Shetland to be with Eldon at their father's memorial service, the body as yet still missing off the coast of St Ninian's Bay, the suicide note making things horribly clear. At the same moment the Icelandic Eyjafjallajökull volcano eruptions were shutting down European skies, and on each stop of that long, long journey to Shetland, Elliot was unsure if he'd get on the plane for the next leg. Now, in another moment of chaos and loss, Elliot's half-brother has made a journey in the other direction, unsure at each point if things will go to plan. But Eldon is bright and upbeat and talks enthusiastically about going to university when he gets back, and how he is especially keen to experience the (usually) lively Glasgow music scene. I hope he gets the experience he deserves. Eldon plans to work in Shetland when he graduates. He seems a hundred per cent sure of this; even in this fluid, transitionary moment of growing into adulthood he knows where his home is and where he wants to land. His imagined life has a trajectory, and all of its wheels seem to be firm on the road.

When I read poets from Shetland like Christine De Luca, Roseanne Watt, Jen Hadfield or Robert Alan Jamieson, I recognise a depth of belonging that I once had here, on the flaxy, wild-weather hillsides of Wellington, Porirua and the Kāpiti Coast. The land made sense to me aesthetically and temperamentally. I like a tree sculpted by the wind. I like a rocky seaside with arms of kelp swaying on its surface. It made a kind of order for me, and also left a space for disorder and mystery. I would get homesick when I travelled away. I went to the UK with Kester and Elliot when Elliot was not quite two. We visited Kester's relatives in lovely old homes in Cornwall and Kent, and I was restless and impatient. I couldn't appreciate the moment I was being offered. I found the homes dark and stuffy with their antique furniture. Things felt formal and easily disrupted if you didn't understand the rituals and order of the days.

One day I sat over morning tea with Kester's aunt and uncle. Kester, who should have been there too, was out running, and when he popped his head in the door to say hi and sorry and that he'd be there soon, his shiny face and limbs, his shorts, his sweaty T-shirt, his long hair, felt like a Technicolor gash in a sepia moment. A very New Zealand Technicolor gash. I do remember one elderly relative sitting the pinhead oatmeal on the Aga to slowly warm and cook overnight; how his face was alight as he told me how delicious it would be for our breakfast. And it was. If I wasn't so impatient, so fearful, I might have had many such moments. I might have been able to receive the gifts I was being offered. But I was looking past and through almost everything, I was hungry for a blue or green or grey horizon, a sea horizon, a view that wouldn't bounce back at me because of insufficient room to unfold.

One night I left the living room where we were all sitting and went out into the garden just to breathe. When Kester followed me, I said, *can't we walk to the pub? Why do we have to sit around inside?* I was 26 years old and panicking. I felt as though those graceful old houses of England could cast a spell and keep me there forever. One of Kester's aunts bought a hairbrush and set about trying to make sense of Elliot's mass of ringlets. Good luck, I thought. In the end, Elliot's hair stuck out all around his head in an electrified spray, much wilder than the original curls. I kept an eye out to see she didn't go and buy a pair of scissors. I don't know what the relatives thought of me, but I only really breathed out when we visited friends in London, but even then, not really, because Kester and I knew, in a gentle way, that we were not well matched. Not in all things, anyway, and being with his friends or mine made me feel that we were not really at ease in each other's worlds. We did share a huge love and appreciation for our boy, laughing at his heroic upbeat energy as we dragged him around Europe. I can see him now on his Mothercare trike, cycling along a railway station in Italy at night, proudly leading the way. He had, he has, the famous Wigram energy. But Italy came later.

Things only really fell into place for us in the UK when we went to stay in Kester's godmother's croft in Scotland, above Loch Ness. The croft, which was empty at the time, was on the side of a hill, inside a forest. It was winter, almost Christmas, and a thick snow fell and everything went silent. The holly tree that sat to one side of the front door lifted up its own snow replica, each leaf perfectly sculpted in white, each red berry iced. We all loved it there and relished having a house to ourselves again. Sometimes a deer would come out of the forest and hesitate for a second by the croft before flickering away, like somebody blew it out. Kester could go tramping in the hills. We three could walk to the little local store for our supplies. We were invited to a Christmas celebration for the local children. We lit fires in the big fireplace and read books. Over Christmas dinner – a goose from the nearby farm – Kester and I decided to go to Islay for Hogmanay. He had friends there. The Isle of Islay is the southernmost island of the inner southern Hebrides. Its closest neighbours are the Isle of Jura – five minutes by ferry from Port Askaig at the north end of the island, and Northern Ireland, 40 kilometres south. When we arrived in Islay, the island flew like a spear into my heart, and stayed there – too deeply embedded to remove. If the croft at Loch Ness soothed me, Islay woke me up. All of my self-involved impatience, claustrophobia and homesickness fell away, and I felt myself, finally, listening out.

I am writing this in the herb garden in Wellington's Botanic Garden. It's warmer here than in the little cottage in the lee of Te Ahumairangi. I stand up and look across to the Remutaka range and the Tararuas beyond. The hills, in shades of blue, are layered, each layer paler and more ethereal. The harbour sits flat today, and silver. I scan my body for the uprise of expansive feelings I would once have had looking out at this view, but it's not there. I feel like I have lost a sense. Why can't I connect here anymore? It's not that I can't see its beauty, and it's not even that it has to be all beauty, but it meant something to me once. I hear a grey warbler sing its clear bright descending song. It places me suddenly in a cottage 20 kilometres up the coast, with windows open and this song coming into the room. Tamara is five years old and sitting under the open window making something complicated with paper and glue and glitter, and quietly copying the birdsong, and Elliot is outside, careering down the steep lane on his skateboard. I am standing in the doorway between the living room and the kitchen. The porch door is open. There it is: the ordinary domestic magic in the end of a day. And what magic it was.

I drop my pen and notebook into my 'Emotional Baggage' tote bag and walk into the oldest piece of bush in the Gardens. Big, wide ferns lift and fall, like breathing. A kākā sweeps past me with a kind of scream and the tūī sing. And I stand on the narrow earth path inside it all and go, *What?* And then I go, *I'm here.* And *Hello?* Part of me knows that this, all this, is inside of me now, it's part of my internal landscape. But part of me wants it to still sing to me through the window where I live, up the coast, with my children and a sense of purpose as lovely and as grounded as a fern.

Yesterday I watched a video of meditation teacher Tara Brach interviewing American writer Natalie Goldberg, whose book about writing fiction *Writing Down the Bones* I've used in my teaching for decades. I love the book's energy and urgency and generosity – all of the things, so clearly embodied in herself, that make her such a good teacher. Towards the end of the interview, Tara asks Natalie how the pandemic has affected her, personally and as a writer. Natalie says that, after 35 years of joyful (enviable) writing energy, she almost wanted to let it go. She said that, with the Trump presidency and the pandemic with its horrors and losses, things (meaning?) seemed to fall away. She glances out of the window beside her and says that before the pandemic she LOVED New Mexico, where her home is, and now, she says, shrugging sadly, 'it's a nice place to live'. I guess this is what long-term trauma can do. It can damage your connection with place and meaning, those two things being so deeply intertwined that you can't pull them apart. Long-term trauma can mean you merely shrug towards New Mexico – where once it was a well from which you drew movement and energy. Your loved place is now merely 'a nice place to live', or perhaps even too complicated to live in at all. Shadows creep across the brick path through the herb garden. Time to go back to the cottage and turn the heat on.

I have had two Hogmanays on Islay, about 30 years apart: the first with Kester and Elliot, when Elliot was a toddler, and the second with Tamara. On that first Hogmanay we stayed with our friend Roland at his home, Quartz Lodge, on the Kildalton Estate at the southeast end of the isle. Quartz Lodge was built to prove a point after a 1900 survey report concluded that there was little quartz on the estate. This seems to me a very Islay way of responding to a wrong of some sort: an embodied and irrefutable response which may hardly need a word spoken. Kester, Elliot and I partied for days in rambling houses and at a cèilidh in a village hall, driving over the thin roads through peat moor and forests, rugged up against a light snowfall and biting winds before bunking down each night in the shining white cottage in the woods.

That first Hogmanay we met Fiona and George who live in the heart of the Kildalton Estate, in what had been a farmhouse, then briefly a hotel, and now was a home again. It was a big, slightly shambolic place with a square courtyard at its centre. On their land there was a black castle, still making its original outline against the sky, but crumbling inside with floors fallen through and trees poking at its empty windows. This castle was built by John Ramsey, who took over the lease on the first whisky distillery on Islay when it was struggling – the Port Ellen distillery – that eventually became Laphroaig. He improved infrastructure on the island and was deeply interested and involved in education in Scotland. When the First World War and the following Depression strained family fortunes, the land and its castle were sold to Talbot Clifton, an eccentric hunting and shooting man who, on one of his many travels, dined on mammoth recovered from the Arctic permafrost. His wife, Violet Beauclerk Clifton, wrote a biography of her husband called *The Book of Talbot*, which won the 1933 James Tait Black Prize. Their son, the dilettante filmmaker Harry Talbot de Vere Clifton, squandered much of the family fortunes. He did, according to Wikipedia, give Yeats a piece of lapis lazuli which inspired the poem 'Lapis Lazuli'. So, good for something then. I understand why George and Fiona want to let the ghosts have the castle as it deconstructs itself back into the land.

There are bays and coves and woods on the land, and a fairy hill where the Queen of the Fairies lives. From Fairy Hill you can see across to the lochs and skerries, and beyond to the open sea. Fiona tells me how, some years ago, as part of a major naval exercise the Ministry of Defence installed a microwave transponder at the top of Fairy Hill. They left it there overnight which annoyed George who dismantled the transponder and locked it away in an outhouse, fearful of the effect it might have on the fairies. The following day, out in the Sound, a destroyer and several naval ships languished, unable to proceed with their exercise due to the impounded transponder. After some negotiation the Ministry of Defence wrote a cheque for £120 towards the Islay swimming pool fund and produced the required letter of apology to the Fairy Queen and the confiscated equipment was returned.

Strangely, in terms of what came to pass, Fiona was born in a village called Seal, in Kent. She trained from early childhood as a classical violinist, and then branched out into rock and folk. George was Fiona's manager. He was in love with Fiona and wanted her to start a life with him on Islay. He asked her what her greatest ambition was in terms of her music, and she replied that it was to play at the London Palladium. George organised for Fiona – at 19 – to play at the London palladium as the opening act for Alex Harvey, a Scottish rock and blues musician who had already heard and liked Fiona's music. For the concert she composed what she describes as a Scottish 'Greensleeves'; it was called 'Islay Mist'. She performed in bare feet and a long dress, already halfway to Islay in her imagination.

In Islay, Fiona began composing for and playing to the common and grey seals that frequent the rocky bays on their land. The seals quickly got to know her, and whenever she went down to the bay to play, they would pop their slick dark heads up, turn their huge black eyes to her, and listen. This was not just a lovely, youthful impulse, it was the beginning of an ongoing practice; Fiona has been playing to the seals for decades. She is still playing to them as I write this, despite the aches and pains of older hands. As she plays to the seals, she notices them. She notices seals returning year after year, she notices if a particular seal doesn't turn up, or if a seal pup is parted from its mother, or if one of them looks injured. And along with this communication and noticing, which you could also describe as call and response, or speaking and listening, or just being in relationship, she does coalface activist work to protect them. She and George were founder members of the Islay and Jura Seal Action Group, and work with the RSPB, Greenpeace, Animal Concern and other organisations to protect seals and raise awareness of their plight, including 'culling' by some fishermen. Fiona's connection with and resulting urgent obligation to the seals feels like a lesson right now. Feminist scientist and scholar Donna Haraway talks about having relationships with earth-based creatures, and the earth itself. She calls it making kin, and how there are both enduring obligations and gifts in these relationships. She writes, 'I have a dog, a dog has me.'

The seals have Fiona and Fiona has the seals. She was in Paisley Maternity Hospital, having just given birth to her third daughter, when she had a call from a friend on Islay asking if she could look after an ailing grey seal pup that had been found on Islay's Oa peninsula. Fiona attended the pup in her home in full protective clothing, including a mask to avoid catching any airborne germs. After a week it was eating whole fish – much of its food source donated by local fishermen. As the pup was brought back from the brink of death, the RSPCA Wildlife Hospital in Norfolk offered to take him on so that Fiona could go back to just looking after the one baby, her human kin.

I saw a seal in the bath at Fiona and George's place and the same seal watching television in their living room during that first visit to Islay, when we played and danced at the turn of the year.

At the turn of another year, 30 years later, we were on Islay for Hogmanay again, my grown-up kid, Tamara, and me cycling towards Quartz Lodge, only a little tired after a Hogmanay celebration at Port Ellen Hotel the night before. There was a big fire blazing in the living room at Quartz Lodge, and as we settled in it hit me that, as Roland's first footers, we hadn't brought a piece of coal or any food to offer as good luck for the year ahead. This is an oversight that still makes me cringe; how could I turn up on invitation to someone's home with nothing to offer anyway, but on this day of all days? We scratched around in our backpacks and found half a block of tablet. Good enough. I gave it to Roland hoping that he would always have something sweet in his life and in his belly in 2020. Roland brought through coffee and went back to the kitchen to prepare oat cakes and cheese. While Roland was in the kitchen Tamara stirred sugar into their coffee and the liquid in the cup started to foam and hiss. Tamara whispered to me that it smelt like laundry detergent and expected me to be more surprised than I was. They carried the foaming cup through to Roland who realised he'd set out a bowl of laundry powder instead of sugar. Or the fairies had made mischief for we unmindful first footers.

Roland drove us to see the Kildalton Chapel, which sits on an undulation of moorland with bare trees to one side of it and to the other, the sea. The chapel is roofless with peaked end walls which seem to lift up to the sky in a human-like gesture, held permanent – but the land knows better. Outside the chapel is the 8th-century Kildalton High Cross. A lattice of animal life emerges from the weathered stone. There are lions and snakes and even peacocks. For all of its undoubtedly Christian symbolism, it has a Pagan energy, showing one thing emerging from the other, the little nubbed creatures slightly unmade by time, some looking unborn, or just-born – all long back and large and heavy head. The work of lifting the head up when emerging from a big stone mystery into an airy world felt recognisable. I looked and looked to see which version won, Pagan or Christian, and then allowed that both were there and should be, and, possibly, always were. Let all good magics merge to help connect us to our world. In photos from this day, Tamara and I peer out of puffer-jacket hoods like seals lifting water-slicked faces out of the sea. 2020 had arrived and something was coming that we hadn't seen before. We couldn't imagine it yet or hear it in the distance. As we left Roland's place that day, we stopped to look up at the forested incline behind the cottage, where Roland leaves food for the deer who come down the hill each night to eat the offerings. I imagined the leggy creatures appearing out of the trees at dusk, their light hooves making a rainfall sound.

From Port Ellen towards the Kildalton Estate, you pass three Kildalton whisky distilleries. The first is Laphroaig, by the sea loch, Loch Laphroaig, then Lagavulin sitting at the very edge of Lagavulin Bay, and Ardbeg, pressed to the edge of Loch an t-Sáilein. We stopped at each one of them as we cycled to Roland's place that morning. I walked on rocky edges in front of the sea-facing, white-washed whisky warehouses. They were like long white boats, the name of the distillery in thick black letters along their length. Behind them were the peat kilns with their shapely roofs, like Buddhist temples. We left Quartz Lodge and cycled back the way we came, along the thin road towards Port Ellen, and passed the Kildalton distilleries in reverse order: Ardbeg, Lagavulin, Laphroaig. Some places you pass through and there is no exchange. I passed through Islay, and Islay stained and flavoured me. The weight of my body on the cranky old, hired bike making a hum on the land, which was to me a kind of love song.

Eldon has left New Zealand and travelled to Brisbane – in between travel suspensions – to stay with Elliot and Ret. They are currently in lockdown again as community cases are growing, so they can't go to the beach, but he and Elliot can go climbing in the warm Brisbane evenings at Kangaroo Point, a cliff above the Brisbane River with a sweeping view of the city, and they can go mountain-biking through the open eucalypt forests of Toohey Park where koalas sleep or sleepily look down from high swaying branches. Also, Tamara has bought a section in the Wairarapa, over the wildly steep Remutaka Hill Road an hour or so from Wellington. The section has a big shed on it with a working forge inside. The shed is beautifully half-bricked around the forge. The air in the shed is still and dry and particle-rich, like a church or a boatshed, or my dad's workshop where he repaired and tuned pianos. It is a place where things have been made and unmade and remade into something else. The forge was once used to make a component part for the railway lines of greater Wellington, and then it was used to make horseshoes. Most recently it was owned by John, now in his 90s, who collected local memorabilia, and who showed people around, telling the stories of the different historical pieces, for a two-dollar entry fee. John's son sold the property for him, and he picked Tamara's offer above other higher offers because they had included a letter, telling the owners what their vision was for the place. Tamara is an artist and will make art using the forge. I have put my name down for a made-from-scratch kitchen knife with a native wood handle. The knife will come from the forge that is currently Tamara's and was John's and that made horseshoes and before that, railway lines. Things turning and returning, coming and going as they do.

*

I am standing in the doorways of the houses we have lived, and the islands we have known. The kids are safely making and exploring. The porch door is open. The grey warbler sings its descending scale. There it is, the ordinary magic in the end of a day. And what magic it was.

Eight

Home

Houses

I have been thinking about houses. There is a space where my home should be, and this leaves me feeling tired and exposed. So I am thinking about houses and belonging.

I print out photos of Vida's home, Dunella in Bieldside, Aberdeenshire, and my grandmother's home in Derwent Street, Island Bay, and sit them side by side. I peer closely at Dunella, where Vida and Henry and their two boys lived. It is a handsome two-storey granite house by the Deeside golf course, with a good-sized room for each boy and wide hallways with a grandmother clock keeping shadowy guard. A large shed on the section, with two shining bikes in it. And then I look at the modest bungalow of 39 Derwent Street, where so many of my immigrant family came and went, and where my father grew up, sharing a room with his brother. A fluid but also constant home.

I was raised in a constant home, at 12 Pā Road, Pukerua Bay, until my parents built a house at number 11 Pā Road, and we shifted next door, just a small shuffle along the edge of the gully, with its flax and toetoe and mingimingi and macrocarpas, and at the end of the gully, the sea. Eventually my mother's parents joined us on the edge of the gully, shifting into 13 Pā Road, and because Nana was superstitious, she had to put a spell on the number 13 and make it lucky. Architects lived on the apex of the hill at the very end of our tiny, bushy road, looking straight out over the two small bays and Kāpiti Island; the vantage point that would have made it a good site for a pā.

Most of the homes I lived in with my kids were also in the small seaside town of Pukerua Bay. We lived in houses on steep hillsides, or tucked down in a dip between hills and accessed by a vertical driveway, or at the edge of a gully looking across green waves of flax to the sea. We lived with our toes in the sand in baches (mostly gone now) on the beach. But always, like a great anchor sunk deep into the soil of Pā Road, was my parents' house, the home we circled. Our version of 39 Derwent Street. For a long time we four siblings lived close to my parents and grandparents in Pukerua Bay; we raised a thousand glasses of wine there; we brought new partners and new babies to be admired there. We had parties, we laughed, we commiserated, we sat around the fire that our parents lit in this, the 'new world', with us at its centre.

Was Dunella a constant home? Yes, I think it was constant. It was where Vida and Henry brought their new born babies home. It is where, in a photograph, a very young Vida and her still-young-looking mother play in the garden with the boys on their shoulders. It is where my great-grandparents are photographed with the boys, who are maybe eight and ten, looking handsome in kilts, and holding the handles of two large bikes. Perhaps it is Christmas. Perhaps it is at the start of the war. Perhaps Vida has shifted out and the housekeeper has shifted in. Dunella was the home that Vida comes back to, after the war, after Arthur, after her job, and it is the place, years later, that she left for good, for a life of homelessness. Unlike some of the beach baches that I came and went from, this big stone house is still there. I know this because Margaret took a photo of it for me. It has not diminished or disappeared with time. Margaret tells me that her family shifted to Dunella when Henry was becoming old and sick. They loved the big stone house by the golf course. It was a beautiful house to grow up in, she says. When Henry died, they discovered he had debts and, to their sorrow, Dunella had to go.

Dunella is double-gabled, and upstairs between the gables there is a French door and a balcony. A place to take in the view. To wave to a new husband rushing home from work or a round of golf to his pregnant wife. And later, a place to call out from when you have drunk too much, and they have drunk too much, and you are working from the very lowest part of yourself. The boys in their roomy rooms ducking out to get their bikes and leaving their parents to it. Dunella with its rows of chimneys at either end, the tall, elegant rooms with their long windows, the transom and sidelights framing the heavy front door, the finials to keep witches from landing on the roof and making their way inside.

In the years that Vida was living in and leaving Dunella, her sister, my grandmother, was presiding over sons and a husband and brothers at 39 Derwent Street. My father's constant home. The steps he sat on to teach himself the piano accordion. The Empire picture theatre around the corner where he went to cowboy pictures. The beach down the road where he paddled his canoe to the little island. Scotland just a shape in the mouths and vowels of his parents, and in the colourwork of his mother's knitting. Not a memory of light, but a song. Not a bird, but a story. Not an ache, but the shadow of an ache. Not a love, but a *something*; what to call it, this inheritance? The way you make that gesture of inclining your head when you listen, which your Aunty Janet from Aberdeen, whom you had never met until just now, also makes. One Christmas in Edinburgh I sent my nephew, Gabe, a copy of Roald Dahl's *The Twits* translated into Scots, jokingly setting a challenge for him to read it to his kids. Later he told me that when he started to read it aloud, he found that the Scots words were right there, in his mouth.

When Vida left Dunella to live who knows where, my grandparents went on living at 39 Derwent Street, my grandmother happy and playful sometimes, and other times frustrated by a life that didn't quite happen as she would have liked. Teaching her cockatiel to say 'Good boy Jimmy, bad boy John' for her two sons: the good son, my father, and the naughty son, my uncle, her favourite. I think she had an affair with a pilot. Another half-whisper. In 1946, after the war, the year that Vida remarried Henry, my grandmother is photographed in Wellington in the cockpit of a Tiger Moth plane with a friend. She is wearing a pilot's hat that reminds me of *The Aviatrix*, that Rita Angus painting of her sister wearing her flying helmet. My grandmother looks happy in the photo. Perhaps her friend had been a fighter pilot, like her husband in the previous world war. Later, my grandmother wore a large stylish brooch in the shape of a plane pinned to the collar of her swing coat. At this point, I think, she was close to becoming a character.

In retirement my grandfather, going against public (Johnston) opinion, shifted them to their beautiful home in Otūmoetai in the Bay of Plenty, with its stone-fruit trees framing the driveway; we would smell the squash of them under the car tyres as we arrived for our long summer visit.

Vida left Henry at the start of the war and the boys stayed with their father and the housekeeper in Dunella. In the United Kingdom it was 1973 before women gained equal custodial rights with men. Until then, the father was the legal parent, and mothers only got custody of their children until the age of seven. So, even if she had wanted to take the boys with her, she would have needed Henry's permission. She might have wanted to take them with her, or she might not have wanted to. Each possibility like a piece of land with a network of sea caves beneath it, shuddering and echoing with the coming and going of tides. I do know that years later she took Margaret to *The Sound of Music* when it came out in the mid 1960s. I imagine that Vida had seen it already, and enjoyed the music and the drama of the brave singing family, and wanted her granddaughter to enjoy it too. I imagine the phone call where Vida asks if she can take Margaret out. I imagine the young Margaret putting on her coat and then nervously waiting for Vida, who she hardly knew, to arrive. I imagine Vida glancing at her granddaughter's face during 'Edelweiss' and 'How do you solve a problem like Maria?' Margaret tells me that she remembers another time, a few years later, when she was a young teen working during her holidays at Asda, seeing a woman she thought was Vida working in the staff canteen, but she felt too shy to approach her. Too shy and also pulled in complicated ways by loyalty to her father. I wonder if Vida saw her, this granddaughter who lived in the house that she left.

The last home I find for Vida is Wernham House in Aberdeen, a residential accommodation for adults who have drug, alcohol and mental health problems. People who are, most often, long-term homeless. Wernham House is named after Hilda Frances Wernham, who founded the Aberdeenshire Cyrenians, a charity looking at the causes and consequences of homelessness. I look at the Wernham House website and feel relieved that it looks like a good place, has a good ethos. It is made of the usual Aberdeen granite. I pay for a death certificate for Vida. She died at Woodend Hospital in Aberdeen at 86 years old. Her son took care of the arrangements. There was no formal service, and her name is not engraved in stone, not anywhere that I can find. The last photograph I have of Vida is from a 1986 issue of the *Aberdeen Evening Express*. She is a resident of Wernham House, is in her 70s and is taking part in a walk to raise money to build a shelter for homeless women. She looks strong, broad-shouldered, undiminished.

Homes are where we live. They are the places we launch from, bare feet on twiggy nest edge and off we go, finding our rhythm. They are places we go back to. They are places we are shut out of. Or are trapped inside. They are large encircling arms. They are shared, opening and encircling arms or else they are dead spaces. And yet, there are encircling-arms-homes with dead spaces in them. I have stepped into and out of all of these sorts of homes and spaces.

Vida taps me on the shoulder and says, *'Forget the houses and all of that small beer tribal stuff, what about the castle!'*

The castle

I was staying in a tall pink castle perched on the edge of an escarpment above the River Esk in the middle of a wood, in Midlothian. It was 2013, and I had a Hawthornden Castle Writing Fellowship and was to be living there for a month with five other writers. It was autumn and the trees in the woods around the castle were turning. It was a proper castle, nothing Disneyland about it, despite it being pink and tall and impossibly pretty. An L-plan tower house, the three-storey tower and curtain wall in the courtyard are 15th-century, and the rest is 17th-century. The castle was sacked twice during 'the rough wooing' of the 16th century – the wars between Scotland and England. Sir John Drummond, Gentleman-Usher for King James VI of Scotland, acquired the barony about 1600. Sir John Drummond's son, Sir William Drummond was a poet, and he was visited in 1619 by Ben Jonson, on Jonson's celebrated walk from England to Scotland, and who in the book *Notes of Ben Jonson's Conversations with William Drummond of Hawthornden* is noted as saying that Drummond's poems were good 'Save that they smelled too much of the Schools, and were not after the fancie of the time'. Charles Dickens visited Hawthornden Castle at the height of his fame, but was turned away by the housekeeper who, when he protested 'My good woman, my name's *Dickens*, and I can't come here every day', is believed to have replied, 'I neither ken nor care what your name is, but ye canna get in except on regular days.'

When I arrived at its doors, Hawthornden Castle was owned by Drue Heinz, very old by then and, among other things, an arts patron and former publisher of *The Paris Review*. She bought Hawthornden Castle in 1982, and founded the Hawthornden Castle Writing Fellowship so that writers could have a quiet retreat to do their work, and we particularly bless her memory for that.

For the first few days I wandered around the castle, trying to make an internal map of the place. I stepped across a shapely lawn with an early morning mist hovering like an aura above it. I wandered through a forest where trees had faces and arms and stories. I looked into a deep well at the centre of a triangular courtyard which bordered a steep escarpment, and wondered about health and safety, but I was secretly glad there were deep unguarded wells and low walls above sheer drops and plenty of sherry to drink. It seemed right that the dangers of castle life hadn't entirely been smoothed away. Outside the library, which was just beyond the castle, there was a Victoria plum tree heavy with translucent oval pink and yellow plums. It was an intimate experience to rest one in your palm, warmed as they were by early autumn sun. It was in a stand of trees by the library where I saw a fawn, standing perfectly still, looking at me. It stood still for so long that I wondered if it were actually real. Perhaps it was a forest statue, its dark glossy eyes reflecting mornings and nights, moons and suns. But finally I moved and saw it move and vanish.

One night, we had a formal dinner in the dining room attended by a man in a full kilt – including an otter sporran – who, the following day, was going to the 270th anniversary of the Battle of Culloden. We writers placed ourselves around the long table. I was told that I was sitting where Seamus Heaney had sat only a few months before, with Marie beside him.

There was a spiral stone staircase leading up to our rooms, and after breakfast I would spiral up to my room to write. It was useful to start the writing day with a turning, looking into grey stone, as though someone had blindfolded and turned me to disorient, to shake up the familiar (as much as a castle in Scotland could ever become familiar to me). But this daily twist seemed to send me out to meet the distant relatives who lived at the edges of myself. At night I spiralled up to my room to sleep after too many sherries with my fellow writers in the drawing room followed by a hearty dinner where I, and most of the others, seemed to eat and eat and eat, like we had been hiking all day, and we had not. A few weeks into the residency, I took some days out to go to the British and Irish Contemporary Poetry Conference at the Centre for New Writing at The University of Manchester, where I was to be part of a panel and give a talk on repetition in Kathleen Jamie's poetry collection *The Tree House*. It was strange to leave the castle where I had been spending silent, unbroken days in my room, a wicker basket of lunch left outside my door, to go down the spiral steps and through the woods, back out to the road to catch the bus and then the train to Manchester where I would talk about the poetics of a tree house.

Seamus Heaney was meant to be reading at the conference and I could hardly believe I was going to be in the same room as him, and that I would hear him read his poetry in real life. Heaney was a touchstone poet for me. A favourite end of term gift-poem for my students was Heaney's 'Postscript', one of his many driving poems. I recognised so well the impulse that the poem describes – that moment when you see a view so beautiful you want to stop the car, get out and see it *more*. But 'You are neither here nor there' the poem says. Which always feels pretty accurate. And that just by travelling through the world you will sometimes be floored by it, it will 'catch the heart off guard and blow it open'.

Years back, for an MA in English Literature, I studied Heaney's 12 'Station Island' poems at the centre of his 1984 *Station Island* collection. The poems traced a pilgrimage to Station Island, or St Patrick's Purgatory, to meet, in the circling and the kneeling, his literary and familial ancestors and to listen to their voices again. At the time, the poems and the work saved me. As I plodded an unsacred but surely circuitous path through the Family Court, the 'Station Island' poems were a pilgrimage for me. I went back to them night after night, possibly with bare feet, possibly kneeling, my books laid along the couch. A taupata outside the window would turn its orange berries out, and darkness would pour in. I didn't close the curtains, not even when my children slept in their beds, nor did I shut their door. Let them hear me look into the well and set the darkness echoing, let my murmurings infect them with a strange kind of believing. The press of small transformations.

Heaney died just days before the night that he should have been reading at the conference, and in his place Paul Muldoon gave a beautiful reading that acknowledged the space where Heaney suddenly wasn't, that referenced the poems we weren't hearing him read. He said, for Ireland, it felt that their father had left the room. Yes, I thought when I heard him say that, I feel it too. The next day, on the way back, I got off the bus at Bonnyrigg, a small, plain town a few kilometres from Hawthornden Castle. I wanted to walk the rest of the way, as a transition. I got off the bus beside the community pool. A group of children, maybe five to seven years old, were standing by the door of the centre with two adults. They were waiting for a little girl who was running towards them, apparently late. Her shoes were too big and flapped on her feet. Her long school uniform strained around her belly. Her hair was bright red and her cheeks were a different shade of bright red. She was calling out 'I love after school club! I love after school club!' Part girl, part red-brown hare, she lurched joyfully towards her mates and through the doors, to the pool. With tears suddenly pricking my eyes, I walked, tree by tree, back to the castle.

No house at all

The writing residency is over and I have shut the door on the little Thorndon cottage in Wellington. I am renting a friend's spare room, and I am wondering where I will live now, post lockdown, post Scotland, post residency. I go on the unemployment benefit. I take my creative writing classes. I work on this memoir. Covid is making its way down the island. The question of where next for me feels unanswerable and unmanageable but urgent. And then into this tailspin, the beautiful stillness of grandparenthood. The feeling of *rightness* when my grandchild is born. It is an animal feeling, as if I could flick my tail and disappear into the brush. Some kind of work is done. And then there is the human feeling of just wanting to watch her, my grandchild, re-make the world, by touch, by smell, by breath, by word. So, in an anxious impulse which ignores the fact that I can't live in a humid climate, I decide it would be a good idea to move to Brisbane. I hope that in Brisbane, with my newly expanded family on hand, I might feel safe again. I know that my psychic and emotional safety is not a job I can contract out to other people, I know that very well by now. But right at that stripped back moment, I want to believe in it, because I need to put anxiety down.

Flooded

I arrive in Brisbane towards the end of devastating floods through South East Queensland and Northern New South Wales, during which 22 people drown. In Brisbane, two-storey houses are up to their roofline in untethered rivers, creeks and streams. People climb up into their roof spaces and drown there. People climb on to their roofs to wait for boats to rescue them. When the rain stops there are days of 36-degree heat where the air is soupy with humidity as the drenched land steams. There are whole streets with house-lots of furniture stacked on grass verges waiting to be picked up by council trucks and taken to the dump. At the same moment, Russia invades Ukraine. The marvellous Ukrainian-American poet, Ilya Kaminsky, in one of his many tweets about the war, quotes Brazilian poet Adélia Prado, 'I love you, love you, love you, / sad as you are, O world'. I hardly know where to look, so I don't look. I glimpse and then look away. Over and over. I gaze at my granddaughter, who just shines. The smell of frangipani wafts through all of the open windows. A cane toad sits in the middle of the lawn under a sickle moon. The frangipani tree drops a creamy flower, which floats straight down to the grass where it settles silently, face up. Elliot, Ret and I eat our meals at the long table in the deep covered veranda. The open, light-washed house feels worlds away from the dark, Victorian spaces of the Wellington cottage, and more worlds away from my tenement flat in Edinburgh. In the last two years I have walked into my past and into my future. I am currently carrying the future in my arms. Emily has green-brown eyes and a wide-open gaze. Brisbane is beautiful and steamy and hot up here on the hill. Down in the low areas water sinks into wet earth or pools on earth too sodden to accommodate it and rises up in warm, dense vapours. I feel sick with the heat and humidity and spend days lying on my bed with the aircon running.

I feel like Brisbane, like I am holding too much rain. I'm not quite sure how to clear space to make this imagined new life. I apply for a job working at the State Library of Queensland by putting on a snorkel and bumping against murky things in the brown water and coming up for air. I cry when I finish the application then open one of the documents I attached to the application and it is blank. My statement that addresses the selection criteria has turned invisible. My computer is sodden with its thousands of documents, and stops saving into the proper folders and files. They are saving outside of the places where I think they should go. I don't know how to keep track. The document I am writing this on has saved into a rogue place. I don't know how to hold things together anymore. If I live in Brisbane, near to my son, I miss my kid in Wellington. Yet I was far far away from both of them for those four years in Edinburgh and it was okay. I had it sorted once, in my head, how it worked. How we could be a family from a distance. But I seem to have forgotten. All of the containers are spilling. I am spilling. I drop my face towards my granddaughter's head with its shadow of dark hair, I look at her long black eyelashes, the large foresty eyes of my family, the widows peak and creamy skin of her mother, and breath in.

Brisbane raised its eyebrows at me when I arrived, and seems to grow more impatient with me the more I try to find my feet but stumble. I literally stumble over a stone on a pavement and fracture my ankle. I go to job interviews in a moonboot. In one interview for an admin position in a small law firm, I am asked to join in with a staff game of Pass the Pigs, a board game where the dice are two pigs and your moves depend on how they fall. I know it is a kind of psychological test, and I pass it (pretending to find the game funny, but really finding the whole scene manipulative and uncomfortable). I am offered the job and accept it, then quickly change my mind and turn it down. I am operating at a vast distance from my body. I try to think of ways to ground myself.

I walk in Whites Hill Reserve, just ten minutes from Elliot and Ret's place. I go there in the early hours to miss the gathering hum of heat. The sunlight is more diffuse than Aotearoa's shimmering tinfoil sun and covers way more territory than Scotland's low gold coins. The white Brisbane light touches the gums in the open eucalypt forest: the ironbark, scribbly, ghost, and all the other gums that I don't know, and in their spare and wavery shapes they are like a kelp forest that I am swimming through. I stop at the precious remnant of rainforest, which is ferny and dense, and geckos flicker by my feet. In this small, important reserve are other magical sounding creatures that I haven't seen yet, like powerful owls and sacred kingfishers. There are small bright yellow butterflies flickering above the ground and round black tadpoles wriggling in the creek. The kookaburras get into groups and laugh, and the little black willy wagtail – messenger of good luck or stealer of secrets – lands on a pale branch to the right of me and fans its black tail. I tell it I won't be living in Brisbane for much longer, that this is not my home.

One night coming back from a warm and thundery walk, I stand outside the house that seems to float on its oblong of lawn to watch Elliot dancing with his baby daughter to Fat Freddy's Drop's *Hope for a Generation*.

Not lost, just unclaimed

On the trip back to Wellington almost everything goes wrong, starting with not being able to hug Emily or the others when I leave Brisbane because they all have Covid. I had shifted into a room in a house nearby. On my way to the airport I ask the Uber to stop at their house, and I stand at the gate, and Elliot gets out of bed to wave from the porch. At Brisbane airport I am pulled out of line because my travel pass hasn't downloaded properly on my phone. One man makes me stand somewhere separate and then disappears. I stand there, hot behind my mask. Later, another man comes and looks at my deficient travel pass and lets me join the line again. The flight is very expensive and very long – we go via Auckland. I think my luggage is booked through to Wellington but it isn't. I go to board my Wellington flight from Auckland and my luggage hasn't been checked on. I miss the flight, and in my moonboot I clomp out of the domestic terminal to find the bus that will take me back to the overseas terminal so I can locate my luggage and check it through. When I find the bus that will take me back to the overseas terminal, someone is getting off with what looks like my luggage (two suitcases, one blue, one purple). At this point I completely lose my mind, in a proper, unarguable way. I insist this is my luggage and there should also be a box of books, and *where is it*, and as I am lost in this fantasy, the true owner of the luggage quietly takes his bags and goes away. Still clinically insane, I report the loss (the theft!) of my luggage to the lost luggage people who explain to me that that was not my luggage. My luggage will be in the unclaimed luggage department in the overseas terminal. Of course it will. I am suddenly horrified and ashamed by my crazy response. It tells me that I am pushed past what I can cope with. It tells me that I could do with some help. When I get to the baggage claim area at the far end of the international terminal, I'm told that because I have left my luggage unattended, they now have to open and inspect it, and this will take some time. I clomp back to the food court where I have the choice of McDonald's or McDonald's. I finally get to Wellington, with a broken foot and a large abscess brewing above my front tooth. Tamara picks me up. The place where I was going to stay doesn't work out because they have just had Covid and are exhausted, and probably also because I'm clomping through their house in a moonboot, looking distressed. I find another place and can finally hang my clothes in a wardrobe and sit still. I can go to the dentist. I can see my therapist and say to her, 'What was I thinking?' And, 'What shall I do now?' And then, in a gold-star therapy move, I answer my own question: 'I am going to build my life again, in Scotland.'

When I am a little recovered, some weeks after getting back to Wellington, I catch the bus to Island Bay to rest against the sea wall and look out to sea. This is my favourite therapy, well, second only to actually being in the sea. Then I decide to go and look at the old Island Bay home. I round the corner from the refurbished Empire Cinema to 39 Derwent Street and find that the house is being demolished. The corner of the house that had the little window seat with the curtain, the one I imagined my father sitting in to read comics and daydream, is torn away, and through that once private space I can see into the living room where my ancestors would sit. I am there just in time to say goodbye. I think of Dad as a boy, sitting on the steps at the front of the house teaching himself to play the accordion. Goodbye diligent and impassioned little boy. Goodbye. Goodbye young man who dances with my mother at the local hall. Goodbye enduring love story. Goodbye father of four. Tuner and repairer of pianos. Goodbye, musician, goodbye, goodbye.

Vida speaks

I was an outlier. Like Mary Queen of Scots I liked to dance and I liked to have an opinion. You can laugh. And yes, I know she was the mother of King James the witch-maker. Home, by the way, is shape and light. It's resonance. But you know that. It's not a contest, it's a feeling. I never wanted to stay in New Zealand. I knew it wasn't for me from the moment I set my foot down in Auckland. Anyway, all that way, those endless oceans, and for what? No, there was never any wrestling for me between the thistle and the fern. Since I've been dead I've been interested in form, this couch for instance, your face, this painting of a jug and bird, the sash window, that wych elm coming into leaf, and formlessness, the memory of my mother, your memory of your mother, the Scotland your father never came to visit, couldn't know. He, a musician, would have known that no country is a lump of dirt; a country is songs and weather and architecture, land shapes and stories and traditions. Form and formlessness. The space between that body and this. Form and formlessness, Lynn. You and me. The living and the dead.

Fairy tale ending

My home is from a fairy tale in an old cloth-covered hardback that I once thought was true. Then for years and years I stopped believing and during that time I was embarrassed to have ever believed in a faraway land from long ago. And then one day the world shuddered and tripped and there I was in the Old Town and Vida was walking towards me, coming back from somewhere – I was up early and she was up late – and we began to skirt each other, but the air was heavy with sirens punctuated by silence, and particle-heavy with disturbed air from all of the running to lock up shops and pubs and museums and art galleries and tourist dungeons and hotels and Fringe headquarters before turning on a heel to run home, and we wavered in the disturbed air and bumped shoulders. The whole of the Royal Mile felt recently vacated, like birds had flown off the sea, poured up its cobbled canyon to shelter in its sea-stack buildings. Our arms lifted and fell as we acknowledged each other. Then she stepped around me. But I followed her. She laughed my grandmother's husky laugh. I followed her past my building, left along South Bridge, past Spoon, Jordan Valley, the bus stop, the Old College, and on until somewhere between the Surgeons' Hall and the charity shops, I lost her. And when I was back in my flat looking out of the kitchen window, in all the shocking gone-ness of that day, I hear her. *The place remembers us, or else it doesn't*, she says. But then I knew that.

Acknowledgements

Many thanks to Lynn Jenner, Elizabeth Knox and Joan Fleming for reading, and giving me excellent feedback on, various versions and parts of this work. Thanks to Lorrane Borwick and the Granton Library Creative Writing Group for allowing me to write about the work we did together, and thank you Marnie Love for permission to publish your poem. Thank you Janet Brunton and others from the Edinburgh & London Poetry Club for your very good company and for allowing me to write about some of the fun we have. Thanks to the women's writing collective, *12*, for being a lovely and inspiring writing community. Thanks to Roland Worthington-Eyre and Fiona and George Middleton for making me so welcome on Islay. Thanks to Susan Price for the gift of books by Mollie Hunter. Thanks to Jules Bradbury and Jane Goldman for friendship, good talks and the last supper. Thank you Jennifer Williams, poetry goddess and friend. Thanks to Alan Gibson and Bruce Carpenter for two housesit/writing residencies in your lovely home. Thank you Lani Murphy, for your wisdom and generosity. Thank you Pier Tosta, for the support, encouragement and good conversation. Many thanks to Margaret Parkinson for so kindly sharing memories, memorabilia and photographs. A big thank you to Alyson Hallett, who I met in a castle and whose friendship helped me to set up my life in Scotland. And thanks to New Zealand-Berliner Hinemoana Baker for the friendship and the fun. Many thanks to Fergus Barrowman and Te Herenga Waka University Press for publishing *Do You Still Have Time for Chaos?* and for continuing to support my work. Grateful thanks, also, to Ruby Leonard for her work editing and typesetting my book. Heartfelt thanks to Jules Bradbury for the beautiful cover art. Thank you and love to Elliot, Ret and Emily Wigram for the beautiful roof over my head in Brisbane.

A special thank you and love to Tamara Friedmann, whose support at a crucial moment allowed me to take time out from my job and begin writing this memoir. I am very grateful for the Creative New Zealand Randell Cottage Writing Fellowship that provided me with the time and (beautiful) space to finish it.

All quotes from Jessie Kesson's *The White Bird Passes* reproduced with permission of Johnson & Alcock Ltd. Quotes from Margaret Tait's *Poems, Stories and Writings* reproduced with permission of Carcanet Press Ltd. Quotes from Fiona Watson's *Macbeth: A True Story* reproduced with permission of Quercus Editions Ltd. Quotes from Sylvia Federici's *Witches, Witch-Hunting and Women* reproduced with permission of PM Press, and quotes from *A Spell in the Wild: A Year (and Six Centuries) of Magic* reproduced with the permission of Dr Alice Tarbuck. The poem 'My People' was reproduced from *Hebrew Ballads and Other Poems* by Else Lasker-Schüler, translated by Audri Durschlag and Jeanette Litman-Demeestere, by permission of the University of Nebraska Press. Copyright 1981 by The Jewish Publication Society of America. Originally published in German as *Gedichte 1902-1943*. Copyright 1959 by Kösel-Verlag GmbH & Co, München.

Essays and poems from this memoir have been published in *Room To Write: 20 years of Randell Cottage writers*, The Cuba Press, Wellington, 2022; *New Writing Scotland 40*, Association for Scottish Literature, Glasgow, 2022; *The Incompleteness Book II*, Australasian Association of Writing Programmes, Recent Works Press, Canberra, 2020; *Strong Words 3: The Best of the Landfall Essay Competition*; Otago University Press, Dunedin, 2023; and verbwellington.nz.

Bibliography

12: A collective of women writers. https://12poetry.wordpress.com

Bloom, Harold (2020). *Macbeth: A Dagger of the Mind*. Simon & Schuster, New York.

Campbell, Marion (1995). *Argyll: The Enduring Heartland*. Lomond Books, West Lothian.

Cusk, Rachel (2020). *Coventry: Essays*. Faber & Faber, London.

Cusk, Rachel (2021), *Second Place*. Faber & Faber, London.

Federici, Silvia (2018). *Witches, Witch-hunting, and Women*. PM Press, Oakland.

Ferrante, Elena (2008). *The Lost Daughter*. Translated by Ann Goldstein, Europa Editions, London.

Frame, Janet (1957). *Owls Do Cry*. Pegasus Press, Christchurch.

Gibbon, Lewis Grassic (2006). *Sunset Song*. Canongate Books, Edinburgh.

Hyde, Robin (1984). *A Home in This World*. Longman Paul, Auckland.

Jonson, Ben (1842). *Notes of Ben Jonson's Conversations with William Drummond of Hawthornden: January M.DC.XIX*. Shakespeare Society, London.

Kesson, Jessie (1996). *The White Bird Passes*. Black and White Publishing, Edinburgh.

Lasker-Schüler, Else (1959). *Hebrew Ballads and Other Poems*. (A. Durschlag and J. Litman-Demeestere, Trans.). Kösel-Verlag GmbH & Co, München.

McDonald, Georgina (1954). *Grand Hills for Sheep*. Whitcombe and Tombs, Christchurch.

MacLeod, Donald (1893). *Dumbarton, Ancient and Modern*. Maclure, Macdonald & Co., ornamental printers to the Queen; Bennett & Thompson, Glasgow.

Manhire, Bill (2003). *Under the Influence*. Four Winds Press, Wellington.

Mansfield, Katherine (1988). *In a German Pension*. Century Hutchison New Zealand, Auckland.

Mantel, Hilary (2020). *Mantel Pieces*. Fourth Estate, London.

Middleton, Fiona (1995). *Seal*. Mainstream Publishing, Edinburgh.

Munro, Neil (1999). *The New Road*. Black and White Publishing, Edinburgh.

Ní Ghríofa, Doireann (2020). *A Ghost in the Throat*. Tramp Press, Dublin.

Robinson, Marilynne (2020). *Jack*. Farrar, Straus and Giroux, New York.

Rose, Jacqueline (2018). *Mothers*. Faber & Faber, London.

Shepherd, Nan (2011). *The Living Mountain*. Canongate Books, Edinburgh.

Tait, Margaret. Ed: Sarah Neely (2012). *Poems, Stories and Writings*. Carcanet Press, Manchester.

Tarbuck, Alice (2020). *A Spell in the Wild: A Year (and Six Centuries) of Magic*. Two Roads, London.

Watson, Fiona (2011). *Macbeth: A True Story*. Quercus, London.

Williams, Terry Tempest (2012). *When Women Were Birds: Fifty-Four Variations on Voice*. Picador, New York.

Woolf, Virginia (1925). *Mrs Dalloway*. Hogarth Press, London.